HOW
SMART PEOPLE
CAN STOP DOING
STUPID THINGS

RON JOHNSTON

For more information about M.O.S.T. or to contact Johnston & Associates, Inc. please visit Johnstonandassoc.com

ISBN: 978-0-692-62365-7

10 9 8 7 6 5 4 3 2 1

Printed and bound in the United States of America

ACKNOWLEDGMENT

I care deeply about the safety of my family, as I'm sure you do too. There are ten primary reasons for making this book happen: my wife, Carol; our children and their spouses, Larisa and Phillip, and Joey and Meleah; and our grandchildren, Lily, Sophie, Sophie Grace, Evey, and Mary Bradley. Each one holds a significantly special and precious place in my heart. I want to share all I know about safety so that they can live safe and productive lives. It is my hope that as a result of reading this book, you and your family may live safe and productive lives too.

Most importantly, a special thanks goes to my wife, Carol, who puts up with me when I become "Mr. Safety" and also patiently tolerates my personal shortcomings when I fail to do everything as safely as possible. She has been my champion, my motivator, and my toughest (and most helpful) editor throughout the writing process. I also have her to thank for the book's title, which she shared with me when all of this was just a stack of notes. When I first mentioned the idea of writing a book, she said the same thing she did when I left the security of a corporate job to start my own company: "Go for it." I am truly grateful that in our partnership we have been able to share risk taking, endure moments of stupidity, and live life fully.

And finally, this book would not have been possible without input from the smart, professional, and seasoned claims adjustors, loss control staff, and leadership at my company, Johnston & Associates, Inc., who kindly shared their wisdom and stories to help the M.O.S.T. principles come to life. I'd also like to thank Betsy Snyder, who helped me organize my ideas in book form so that I can share the stories and strategies of Method Oriented Safety Thinking: The M.O.S.T. System® with people outside of the workplace.

Disclaimer
The messages and lessons in these stories come from real-life situations that I have either encountered personally or have heard about in my many years as a safety professional. In order to protect the privacy of others, some of the real names, events, and details have been changed.

CONTENTS

INTRODUCTION

WHY DO SMART PEOPLE DO STUPID THINGS?

How often have you said, either aloud or to yourself, "I can't believe I did something so stupid"? Maybe you locked the keys in the car at the gym or jumped in the pool with an expensive cell phone in your pocket. Maybe it was something bigger, like backing into your spouse's car while it was parked behind yours in the driveway. You're a smart person, right? So how in the world did that stupid thing just happen?

Unfortunately, "stupid" mistakes often end with more than a ruined cell phone or a locksmith's bill. Many times the result is serious injury, permanent disability, and even death. Even though we intend to be careful, we all do stupid things that leave us embarrassed (at best), hurt, or even worse.

For some people, these stupid mistakes turn into major international blunders that go down in history as some of the most notorious stories of mishap and missed communication.

For example, did you know that during the failed 1961 military invasion of Cuba known as the Bay of Pigs campaign, U.S. military and CIA planners overlooked the fact that Cuba was in a different time zone than their airbase in Nicaragua? The time difference became a major factor in the mission's failure. Or that in 1989, an East German politician by the name of Gunter Schabowski mistakenly lifted travel restrictions between East and West Germany much earlier than planned? He was unprepared to speak publicly on the new policy, and when asked when it would begin, he didn't have an answer; in his confusion, he shocked his colleagues by saying, "Immediately, without delay." Guards had no choice but to open the gates to avoid riots, and the wall came down much sooner than expected—all because Mr. Schabowski didn't take the time to read a briefing carefully before stepping up to the podium.

Some public blunders make headlines because they come with a hefty price tag, like NASA's Mars Orbiter. When the spacecraft took flight in 1999, NASA had used the metric system to build the spacecraft, while Lockheed Martin used the English system of measurement to build the satellite. The discrepancy resulted in the Orbiter being lost in space, and NASA was out $125 million.

Fortunately for most of us, our mistakes, blunders, and general stupidity are unlikely to make international news (thank goodness!). However, one poorly planned action or bad decision can significantly alter the course of our own lives when injury, financial catastrophe, or relationship damage is a consequence.

Humans are strange creatures. We're brilliant enough to invent the Internet and get to the moon, but we're also really good at being stupid. We often and repeatedly set ourselves up for disaster, both in the short and long term. We say stupid things like "Look, no hands!" and take stupid risks thinking, "It won't happen to me." Millions of hours of research have been poured into figuring out why we do what we do. How does it all fit together? How can we be so smart and so easily do stupid things at the same time?

One of the smartest people I've had the pleasure of knowing was my friend Tom, who had spent an entire career in the insurance business. Like me, Tom was no stranger to accident stories. However, when it came to home repairs, he preferred to muscle through a problem instead of hiring professionals for even the toughest tasks. One evening he was hanging shelves in his basement, trying to finish the job and free up the rest of his weekend for golf. He considered calling his next-door neighbor to help him lift a heavy sheet of thick plywood, but he knew the neighbor was out for the evening; completion became his number one goal, and nothing would stand in his way. As Tom reached one hand under the panel and lifted, his bicep muscle tore painfully from his elbow joint. Needless to say, his golf plans for the weekend were postponed indefinitely. How did a brilliant man who heard nothing but accident stories day in and day out in his insurance career make such a stupid decision?

From doctors in hospitals, lawyers in the courtroom, and truck drivers on lonesome highways to nurses in busy nursing homes, politicians on or off the stump, salespeople, pilots, and often the hardest workers of all—stay-at-home moms—not one of us is born with the natural ability to avoid doing stupid things.

Let's face it: we're all going to screw up from time to time. From Adam and Eve to our current political leaders, the pages of history tell the stories of very bright people making very big mistakes. Mistakes are a byproduct of trying something new, and they teach us important lessons that can lead to life-changing discoveries. Just look at Albert Einstein, a genius who made countless mistakes and errors as part of making his profound contributions to our understanding of how our universe functions. He is famously quoted as saying, "Anyone who has never made a mistake has never tried anything new."

> **THE TRICK IS TO KEEP MISTAKES OUT OF THE "STUPID" CATEGORY IN ORDER TO REMAIN PHYSICALLY, EMOTIONALLY, AND FINANCIALLY SAFE AND TO LIVE IN A SAFE ZONE THAT PROTECTS OTHERS, YOUR FAMILY, AND YOURSELF.**

The trick is to keep mistakes out of the "stupid" category in order to remain physically, emotionally, and financially safe and to live in a safe zone that protects others, your family, and yourself.

Einstein also said, "Insanity is doing the same thing over and over and expecting different results." We must train ourselves to learn from our own mistakes and the missteps of others.

Even as a safety professional and the author of a book on the subject, I'm just as prone to doing stupid things as anyone else. That's what drives my passion for safety and accident prevention in the first place.

In fact, many of the stories you're about to read (all of which are true, though some details have been changed to protect privacy) involve either myself or some of the people who have shaped my ideas about safety and stupidity early on, like my kind, supportive mother; my cautious, by-the-book father; and my risk-taking granddaddy.

My mother taught me first and foremost that everyone makes mistakes. Though I know I caused her endless worry and frustration as a rambunctious child, even her strict punishments and stern lectures were fueled by her unconditional love for me and her desire to keep me safe and healthy. Her gravestone's epitaph reads, "A life of caring and doing for others," and it is in this spirit that I share these stories and strategies with you.

My father was a naval aviation mechanic who strongly believed that "There's one way to do it, and that's the right way." On the other hand, my Granddaddy Pierce filled me with an adventurous spirit and a love of excitement; his life's motto was, "There's more than one way to skin a cat." Where Granddaddy taught me to grab life by the horns, my dad pulled me back down to reality and helped me stay on the straight, narrow, and safe path. His credo was that you ALWAYS did things the right way. The two of them (and their opposite natures) had a lot to do with my development of the M.O.S.T. system.

My grandfather enjoyed his more carefree life and seemed to thrive on the thrill of his adventuresome personality. Personally, I wanted to find a way to maintain the excitement and happiness of a life well lived without becoming weighed down with a burdensome "there's only one way to do things" mentality. My father's emphasis on doing things correctly earned him the reputation of always producing quality work, and that reputation provided him with great satisfaction. Because of his careful and exacting nature, my father experienced few accidents in his life. On the opposite end of the spectrum, because my grandfather was so casual about safety as he went about his adventures, he got hurt a lot and made many missteps (with plenty of consequences) that could have easily been avoided throughout his life.

THE ACCIDENT THAT STARTED IT ALL

My own fascination with the cause-and-effect nature of life can be traced back to a sunny day in the early 1950s, an era before seatbelts, bike helmets, and many other safety features we now take for granted. Our family was packed into the car, headed to a swimming hole near our home in Georgia, when we suddenly became the first people on the scene of an awful gas tanker wreck. The truck was completely flipped on its side on the two-lane highway, a tragic one-vehicle accident.

I still remember seeing the steam coming up around the engine and the tires on the high side still turning. It was like the world was in slow motion. We could see a man lying spread-eagle about fifty feet in front of the truck. One of his legs was bent back across the other, and it looked like a bone was sticking out through his pant leg. His head was twisted around at a funny angle. My brothers and I were completely terrified and fascinated at the same time.

My daddy pulled over to the opposite side of the road and very firmly told us kids to stay in the car. He ran to the man and then came back to our car and grabbed one of our swim towels from the trunk. He crossed the road again, more slowly this time, to cover the body. We waited for what seemed like forever for the police to come.

After Daddy talked to the officer and we were on our way again, he was very quiet despite our rapid-fire questions. He gave just one answer to all of our "whys" and "hows," saying, "I guess he was just going too fast for the curve and lost control."

The idea that going too fast and losing control—which I did on my bike all the time—could end so horribly was an idea I couldn't shake. The image of the dead truck driver on the side of the road has stayed with me all my life.

Since then, I've witnessed and investigated hundreds of work-related fatalities and serious accidents. I've pieced together the stories of lost eyes, limbs, and lives. I've watched families absorb the ripple effect of a breadwinner gone too soon and seen the impact of head injuries that changed lives dramatically and permanently.

In every single accident case I investigate, the people involved fixate afterward on what one thing could have been done differently to prevent tragedy. Looking back, it always seems so simple! If only he'd locked out the power first, if the ladder had been steadied, or if she'd taken the extra time to double-check the machinery. It became my mission to find a way for people to live in the present with the same level of clarity they seem to have in hindsight.

In other words, I've spent many, many years of my life studying safety and stupidity and have dedicated my career to finding ways to figure out **How Smart People Can Stop Doing Stupid Things.**© My work led me to develop the M.O.S.T. system, a proven safety training system that focuses on the bigger picture of developing habits informed by risk and human behavior.

I know, I know. Safety training sounds boring and nitpicky. Hearing those words together can make you feel like you're about to be corrected. I'm here to tell you it doesn't have to be that way. This book is about learning to avoid accidents, from small cuts to fatal car crashes, simply by changing the way you think and by forming new habits.

Does living safely mean living in fear or missing out on all the fun? No! Safety isn't a negative force that limits what you can do. I believe it's a positive force that lets you lead a fuller life. Living safely simply means developing habits and behaviors that become a central part of who you are, how you think, and how you act in order to "keep all your fingers and toes," even in risky situations.

ACCIDENT PREVENTION IS ONLY THE BEGINNING

The concepts in this book also apply the idea of safety to all areas of life: making sound decisions, thinking ahead to avoid consequences, and setting yourself up for good outcomes personally, financially, and professionally. When we think about the big picture, "keeping all your fingers and toes" can also describe the need to keep your nest egg intact, keep your relationships healthy, or keep your career on track.

This book will teach you to approach safety like an internal personal insurance policy that follows you everywhere you go, from work to home and everywhere in between. You buy an insurance policy for your house, car, and other valuables. Why not create "free" coverage for your own safety? This is how Method Oriented Safety Thinking® works. It teaches us to think about safety and doing the right thing all the time—essentially, having our own backs by looking before we leap—no matter what.

STORIES, STATS, AND STRATEGIES

Injuries are one of the leading causes of death in the United States. Every day of every year, more people die from accidents than from all diseases combined; every twenty-four hours, over one million people are injured and close to 500 die from accidents. Accident statistics differ with age. For example, auto accidents are the leading cause of teen deaths in the United States, with texting while driving contributing heavily to that statistic; for the elderly, falls are the most common cause of accidental death.

SAFETY ISN'T A NEGATIVE FORCE THAT LIMITS WHAT YOU CAN DO. I BELIEVE IT'S A POSITIVE FORCE THAT LETS YOU LEAD A FULLER LIFE.

Along these lines, I'd like to tell you a story. Amy was an honor roll student, involved in her church youth group, a frequent babysitter in the neighborhood, and an all-around good kid. She knew all about the dangers of texting and driving. Her parents made sure to talk about it often as she worked toward getting her license, and she'd even done a presentation on the dangers of distracted driving as a school project. One evening, as she was driving by herself to a friend's sleepover a few neighborhood blocks away, she took her eyes off the road for just a few seconds to text "On my way" in response to her friend, a person she would see in just a few minutes' time. In doing so, she swerved just enough to hit a police officer as he was helping another driver change a tire on the side of the road. The officer died instantly, leaving Amy to face manslaughter charges that would alter the course of her life forever. How did a good, smart kid make such a horrible mistake? Just once is all it takes.

After reading Amy's story, do you even remember the statistics you read? Statistics are important because they help us identify trends and issues that need attention; I'm just not a big believer in their value when it comes to changing behavior because they're not personal. Numbers and trends simply don't touch us like stories do. In fact, the opposite is often true with statistics: we think, "Well, that's not me. I don't do that," just like how Amy didn't ever text and drive.

Let's take another look at that "500 deaths every day" number. That means that every day, accidents kill the equivalent of two commercial passenger planes full of people. Now imagine if every single day, the news reported two more planes crashing, killing all 500 people on board. Talk about a national crisis! We would immediately, as a country, start looking for a solution (and probably stop flying altogether until we found one). Unfortunately, when those same 500 accident scenes are spread out over 319 million people in the US, they just don't make the same impression.

Statistics are great for showing us that smart people all over the world are making stupid decisions that lead to accidents every single day. However, they also let us think we're above practicing stupidity in our own lives.

So the impact of a personal story like Amy's should hit home and change behavior in the long-term, right? Unfortunately, that's not the case. I observe this all the time in my work. For the first few days and weeks after a shocking workplace accident, everyone on the job is extremely safety conscious. People talk about what happened, how it happened, and how it won't happen again. Forklift drivers wear their seatbelts again. Everyone remembers to put on safety glasses without having to be reminded. Safety procedures are meticulously followed.

Sadly, emotional impact just isn't enough to permanently change behavior. As the weeks and months pass, the old habits begin to creep back in. Supervisors have to stay on their employees for safety procedures and eventually start writing people up and handing out suspensions for safety violations. Ultimately, someone else gets hurt.

We're back to our original question. If statistics don't change behavior and even tragic wake-up calls fade over time, what does it take for smart people to stop doing stupid things? I created the M.O.S.T. system to help solve that very problem.

"The two most common elements in the universe are hydrogen and stupidity." —Harlan Ellison

The dictionary definition of stupidity is "behavior that shows a lack of good sense or judgment." I do realize that using the word "stupid" as often as I do in regard to human behavior has the potential to send the wrong message. The word stupid can be a terrible and hurtful word and is not intended to be offensive here. I would never label a person who has been hurt or killed in an accident as stupid. When I talk about stupidity, I'm talking about what happens when truly smart people make unwise decisions or take actions that seem to go against their better judgment. We've all been there at one time or another.

COMMON EXAMPLES OF STUPIDITY

- A grandfather holding his two-year-old grandson on his lap while mowing grass with a bush hog

- Buying a new house without a professional home inspection

- Trying to find a gas leak with a match

- Putting all of your financial "eggs" in one basket without diversifying investments

- Texting and driving

- Driving a vehicle while intoxicated

- Riding in a car without fastening your seatbelt

- Quitting a job in anger, with no backup plan

- Standing on a rolling chair to change a light bulb

- Leaving a young child alone in a car for "just a minute" to run an errand

- Continuing an unhealthy diet after a health scare, despite doctor's recommendations

HOW TO USE THIS BOOK

Over the years, I've conducted hundreds of M.O.S.T. training and safety classes in many different work environments, from small nursing homes to giant manufacturing plants. I can't even tell you how many times someone has come up to me after a session and said, "You really need to write a book." At first, I laughed it off as a compliment, but after a while I started feeling the push to share my passion outside of my training sessions.

This book isn't a substitute for Method Oriented Safety Thinking® training, but it does contain many of the stories and ideas that helped to shape the system. I wanted to make the behavioral strategies and guiding principles of M.O.S.T. accessible to everyone, not just the people I talk to in the workplace. M.O.S.T. was developed to keep people safe on the job, but it also applies to career and financial decisions, personal relationships, parenting, and all areas of life.

M.O.S.T. WAS DEVELOPED TO KEEP PEOPLE SAFE ON THE JOB, BUT IT ALSO APPLIES TO CAREER AND FINANCIAL DECISIONS, PERSONAL RELATIONSHIPS, PARENTING, AND ALL AREAS OF LIFE.

Just as a factory supervisor should be mindful of his or her own habits when training a new employee, parents must also be intentional about their safety habits in front of the children who are looking to them for guidance. Just as a doctor must consider multiple health issues, medication indications, and a long list of symptoms when prescribing medication for a patient, a first-time car buyer must be aware of interest rates, consumer reviews, mileage, and resale value when making a wise purchase. And just as a distraction on the job can lead to unintended disaster, allowing distractions to block your focus on the needs of family and loved ones can lead to broken relationships.

At the end of each chapter, you'll find a "Stupidity Stopper" section that sums up the lessons and messages you've just read, with simple "Smart Move" suggestions for putting M.O.S.T. into practice. Use these sections as reminders, teaching tools, and quick reference guidelines at home or on the job.

Longfellow was right in declaring, "Sometimes we may learn more from a man's errors than from his virtues." This book is designed to tell the cautionary stories of others' accidents, injuries, and missteps and also to share the safety strategies I've developed in my experience as a risk management consultant. It is my hope that the easy-to-follow ideas outlined here will help you learn to practice safety, not just in certain situations but as a way of life, and that you'll share the knowledge and stories with others too.

This book is also for parents who want to help their children develop safe habits, supervisors who want to protect their employees, and individuals who want to lead a safer, more confident lifestyle. This book is for YOU.

CHAPTER 1

ACCIDENTS JUST HAPPEN
(OR DO THEY?)

I believe it's unrealistic to claim (as many risk management professionals do) that all accidents can be prevented. After all, we live within a world of completely natural forces that cause unplanned and dramatic consequences: weather, for example, or even something as constant as gravity. Think of how many times over the course of your life you've slipped, tripped, or fallen. Every second that you're walking on two feet, you're putting yourself at risk for falls; statistically, it's going to happen, just as there are times when people legitimately find themselves in the wrong place at the wrong time. There are acts of God, unexplained phenomena, and one-in-a-million occurrences happening all over the world every day. Compared to the number of preventable accidents, however, these out-of-the-blue accidents are pretty rare.

THE MYTH OF BEING "ACCIDENT PRONE"

We all know someone we describe as being accident prone, or having bum luck, meaning things seem to just happen to them. From embarrassing mishaps and fender benders to big losses and major catastrophes, they seem to be a walking representation of Murphy's Law. We're always affected by their funny mix-ups, sad stories, and tragic tales, but we're rarely surprised by the situations they get themselves into—after all, accidents just happen to them all the time, right?

In 1995, one of my peers suffered a huge head-smack moment that made a big impression on me. Dave was a respected attorney in our community and someone I knew from church; I'd always enjoyed his company when we were together and felt we had a lot in common. Right before Christmas that year, a childhood friend presented him with a business deal that had the potential to make him a very rich man almost overnight—that is, if he was willing to take a very big risk. His financial planner cautioned him against it and so did several of our peers. Dave gave it some thought and then willingly tossed all of our counsel and concerns (and I suspect, his own gut instinct) completely out the window. He went for it.

Dave poured an enormous chunk of his hard-earned money into an extremely risky oil drilling startup venture in Texas that, had it gone well, could have earned him millions of dollars each year for the rest of his life. Sadly, it really was too good to be true. The well went dry in a matter of months, costing him most of the retirement savings he'd worked his entire professional life to build.

To say Dave lost sleep over the bad decision is an understatement. He allowed the situation to eat away at him for years to come, which affected the way he lived both his professional and personal lives. Later, he told me that if he had a dollar for every time he thought about the moment he signed on the dotted line, he'd have earned all of his money back and then some. Dave was hard working. Smart. Successful. And living proof that stupidity can happen to anyone.

You, me, Dave, and everyone in the world—we all share the same scientific label Homo sapiens, meaning "human." Unfortunately, we also share the same frailties and potentials for a little stupidity here and there along the way. The ability to think for ourselves can certainly protect us from doing stupid things, but it also allows us the freedom to make both good and bad decisions.

In the Bible, the apostle Paul addressed our attraction to stupidity in Romans 7:15, saying, "I do not understand what I do. For what I want to do, I do not do, but what I hate, is what I end up doing." Every one of us has the potential for brilliance and stupidity, and we're in control of which one we exercise.

A safety director shared with me the tragic case of an experienced maintenance mechanic who had worked at the same job for twenty-five years without a serious accident. Ed had several close calls and a few safety violations on his record and had faced disciplinary action by his supervisor a number of times; still, the only accident on his record was this one. Even with years of experience and OSHA training, Ed ignored important safety protocols when he was performing maintenance inside a big electric pulpwood shredder. He switched the blades off before climbing inside, of course, but didn't lock out the main power source, a step that was not only a part of the plant's safety protocol, but a move that should have been second nature given his mechanical experience.

On that day, a newly hired maintenance mechanic had just started his second shift operation. The shredder's conveyor was delivering pulp materials to the mouth of the shredder, but because Ed had stopped the blades, the materials were piling up at the intake slide. The new employee did what he was trained to do and cleared the clog by starting the shear blades. He had no way of knowing there was a man working inside the machine. Ed was killed in just a few horrifying seconds.

Ed had been trained over and over on the OSHA standards of lock-out/tag-out. So why did he take that high-risk chance? How many times had he risked his life doing the same thing before he lost his life on the job? And how about my friend Dave? He also knew the risks of a too-good-to-be-true investment. Why did he bet his life's savings on a deal that was almost sure to fail? Did they just have bad luck, or was it something more?

In most cases, accidents don't happen to unlucky folks like Dave and Ed. Accidents happen because of choices they make. Whether it's in the world of financial management, personal relationships, on-the-job safety, or parenting, people often fail to consider the consequences lurking down each potential path when they make decisions. Instead, they push through at full speed, and eventually, when all hell breaks loose, it's no surprise. I like to describe it as simply recycling stupidity without knowing or realizing it. Accident-prone people seem almost addicted to doing stupid things, even when they know better, resulting in consequences that can seem out of the blue but really aren't.

People sometimes describe themselves or others as being accident prone as if it's a condition beyond their control, in the way that someone is allergic to bee stings or is lactose intolerant. That accident prone label isn't something we're born with. We earn it. When we allow stupidity to build up and repeat itself, we actively create an environment in which it can thrive, and that leads to accidents.

THE TWO CAUSES OF EVERY PREVENTABLE ACCIDENT

Whenever I speak to a group about safety and accident prevention, I ask the audience what causes accidents on the job. Every single time, the two most common answers are "carelessness" and "not thinking."

Those answers are exactly right. No matter what the situation, setting, or circumstance, almost all accidents are caused by carelessness, not thinking, or some combination of the two.

It might sound overly simplistic, but think back to any accident in your life, all the way back to childhood—the time you took a corner too fast on your bike and fell to the pavement or the time you burned your hand on the hot stove because you didn't know it was on. We've felt the effects of carelessness and not thinking our entire lives and will continue to do so until our last days. Fortunately, with awareness and insight, we can also learn to recognize them and take steps to avoid them, eventually as a matter of habit.

CARELESSNESS

Thinking back on my own long list of accidents, I remember my childhood home in Waverly Hall, Georgia, where my brothers and I spent entire summer afternoons rocking ourselves silly in the white high-backed rocking chairs that lined the porch. Even as a kid, I always wanted to fly. It was a dream that fueled my motivation to get my pilot's license as an adult. At age five or six on one summer day, I was intensely daydreaming about flying while I rocked furiously in that old white rocker. Suddenly, the chair tipped forward and dumped me into the bushes in a "tumblesault," as they say in Georgia. I wasn't hurt, but the combination of fear, speed, and loss of control stay with me even now. My carelessness—my distraction and lack of awareness of my surroundings—resulted in my first-ever "flight" and hard landing.

The actual definition of carelessness is the "failure to give sufficient attention to avoiding harm or errors," producing conditions that invite close calls and near misses to happen on a regular basis. Carelessness is dangerous, whether it's a little kid falling off the front porch or Ed climbing inside the shredder without locking out the power source. In our daily lives, we know carelessness by many other names: shortcuts, rushing, taking chances, and not paying attention to our surroundings. It's one of the simplest and most basic causes of accidents yet one of the hardest things to recognize and overcome.

NOT THINKING

Of all my chores, my favorite job as a kid was burning the trash a couple of times a week, usually right after getting home from school. I loved fires: starting them, sitting around them, telling stories, and cooking rabbits and squirrels over them. I didn't mind burning the trash one bit.

As a ten-year-old boy, I knew gasoline was dangerous. One of my favorite wild stories of Granddaddy's involved a burning brush pile that led to an exploding gas can. He used big, dramatic hand motions to show how the can caught fire and burned out of control, with the sides of the can swelling, contracting, and swelling again because of the tremendous pressure inside. I couldn't get enough of the story and asked to hear it over and over.

I had seen adults use gasoline to burn wet brush piles that wouldn't ignite easily. I'd never done it myself, but I knew the gas was thrown from a distance onto the slowly burning fire. I never saw anyone get hurt, and it always worked like a charm.

On one particular day, I wanted to get my after-school chores done quickly so I could play baseball with my brothers. I took a large Tide laundry detergent box from the pile, drenched it with gasoline, and found a book of matches. I thought this was going to be the fastest—and coolest—trash burning of my young life.

I placed the trash bags outside in a ditch we called the "burn pit" and set the Tide box on top, trying to toss lit matches at it from several feet away. Time and time again, the matches went out. By the fourth or fifth match, I was getting impatient and a little bolder. Instead of throwing the match at the box from a distance, I got closer and moved the flaming match slowly across the ragged edges at the opening of the Tide box. It exploded in a terrifying instant, feeding on the fumes that had built up inside the gas-soaked box.

The intense flames and heat caused third-degree burns on my right hand and completely burned off my eyebrows and the front of my hair. The skin on my hand was burned so severely that it sloughed down over my charred fingernails, and I had second-degree burns on my face and arms. Even now, I can't even describe the horrible pain that followed. I'll never forget the nauseating stench of burned flesh and hair or the fear and shock that caused me to sleep for days. I truly thought I was going to die.

ONE OF THE MOST DANGEROUS FORMS OF IGNORANCE IS THE ASSUMPTION THAT WE DON'T SUFFER FROM IT.

Because I was so young, the scars faded over time. The only scar that remains is my own shame: not only did I do something stupid, but I told my parents that the Tide box just exploded on its own and never mentioned the gasoline I'd poured on it. Our preacher even remarked, "It must have been those chemicals they use in washing powder today!"

In my case, not thinking meant attempting something I knew was dangerous without the skills to manage the risk. Sometimes not thinking can simply mean a lack of knowledge—not knowing the right way to do something, using the right tool the wrong way, being trained improperly, or not understanding the consequences of what you're about to do.

I have often heard employees tell stories about times when they've sustained injuries because of not knowing the danger of doing certain tasks. One of those stories involved a mechanic who started working in an automotive body shop where welding machines were in use, producing super bright light. Without knowing the danger, he stared directly at the white-hot blue light and severely burned his eyes. It seemed innocent enough at the time, but the injury was so severe that he had to wear bandages over his eyes for two days in order to recover. In this situation, there was no dedicated or curtained-off area to protect other people in the garage, no warning signs posted, and no supervisor

75 PERCENT OF ALL WORKPLACE INJURIES HAPPEN WITHIN THE FIRST YEAR ON THE JOB.

to give him guidance. So, for this new mechanic, was it stupidity? Not hardly. Not knowing? Absolutely, mixed with a lack of training and an unsafe environment.

Not thinking can be especially dangerous for new employees while they're learning the ropes. Typically, 75 percent of all workplace injuries happen within the first year on the job.

One of the most dangerous forms of ignorance is the assumption that we don't suffer from it. Sometimes, lack of knowledge can actually lead to overconfidence when a fairly unskilled person suffers from the illusion that his or her abilities and skills are higher than they actually are. It's like seeing a professional baseball player hit a home run and thinking, "How hard can it be? He's just swinging a piece of wood!" We'll talk more about the dangers of the "seems easy enough" illusion in Chapter 8.

Let me make one thing completely clear: not thinking is a core cause of accidents, but it is not the same as stupidity. It's when we know we lack the knowledge to do something and do it anyway that stupidity enters the picture, allowing not thinking to join forces with carelessness.

As you read this book, pay close attention in each story to the moment where carelessness and not thinking start to steer the events in a bad direction. Think back on your own accidents, or stories you've heard in your life, and think about the accidents' roots. When we're in tune with the complexity of potential causes behind accidents, we can learn to avoid them altogether by "breaking the accident chain."

BREAKING THE ACCIDENT CHAIN

During an accident investigation, people are quick to point out the obvious cause of a serious accident: falling off of a ladder, failing to shut off power, or not wearing personal protective equipment (PPE). That's rarely the whole story. If we dig a little deeper, we usually find contributing factors that happen prior to the accident itself: fatigue, stress, shortcuts, lack of training, or even preventable mechanical failures.

This sequence of factors is called the "accident chain": a string of moments (often peppered with stupidity) where the many forms of carelessness and/or not thinking link together with mechanical or human factors to determine the course of events, ultimately ending in a preventable accident. Many times, the weak link of the chain of events is held up as the cause of the accident, when in reality, the events and decisions leading up to the accident have just as much to do with the outcome as the weak link itself.

Edward Packard famously created storybooks that allowed the reader to "Choose Your Own Adventure." The books allowed young kids to step into the shoes of the main character and make decisions that altered the plot of the story and ultimately affected the outcome. My own kids read these books over and over again, testing different decisions to see where each path would lead. Sometimes, the character fell off a cliff; other times, he or she found buried treasure or ended up on a rocket ship to Mars.

They were written as children's entertainment, but this book concept is a great example of how the accident chain works. It isn't just one page flip that takes the character into the waiting jaws of a lion. He finds himself there as a result of the series of decisions he made along the way.

Imagine you're driving to a retirement party for a coworker, and you get in a serious car accident that's not your fault. Let's say someone hits your car at a high speed. The impact of the crash sends you flying toward the windshield; your airbag deploys. You, however, had decided not to wear your seatbelt because you didn't want your shirt to wrinkle. Had you been safely restrained, you'd be bruised and shaken but more or less fine. Because you're not wearing your seatbelt, you are violently thrown sideways across the interior of the car, and you suffer a broken spine and a severe head injury that causes irreparable damage to your memory and cognitive functioning. Today wasn't just your coworker's last day of work; thanks to this accident and your new disability, it was yours too.

> **EACH AND EVERY SAFETY DECISION YOU MAKE, WHETHER IT SEEMS SIGNIFICANT OR NOT, AFFECTS EVENTS TO COME.**

Could you have prevented the other driver from slamming into your car? Maybe not, but the accident chain was there long before you collided. It might have started with the other driver being in a hurry, not being aware of his surroundings, or being distracted. Your own accident chain began when you pulled out of the driveway and made the decision to ignore the red seatbelt-indicator light.

This book will help you learn to recognize the links in the accident chain and understand that each and every safety decision you make, whether it seems significant or not, affects events to come. Just like safety glasses, ear plugs, hard hats, hazmat suits, or other forms of PPE protect our physical body from an accident already in progress, the thinking brain can actually provide the greatest level of protection by helping us make the decisions that prevent those accidents in the first place.

When I talk about breaking the accident chain, I'm talking about changing the way we think and therefore the way we act. We can't control all of the links along the way, but by recognizing the buildup of an accident chain and safely changing the links that we can control, we can take steps to keep the ship from sinking, so to speak.

Speaking of ships, it's our common understanding that the "unsinkable" *Titanic* ended up below the ocean's surface because it hit a gigantic iceberg. Actually, the setup for the story's real tragedy—the loss of so many lives—started long before the actual collision. Let's take a closer look at the links in this very famous accident chain:

LINK 1: OVERCONFIDENCE

It's important to note that even before passengers set foot on the giant vessel, it already flaunted the title "The Unsinkable Ship." At the helm was one of the most talented and well-known British captains, embarking on a farewell voyage planned as a celebration of his long and successful career. Captain John Smith was likely operating under a false sense of security as he attempted to set a new speed record.

LINK 2: CARELESSNESS IN CONSTRUCTION

Unknown to the captain and crew of the ship, the design of the ship's hull was fatally flawed. The materials used were weak and substandard. With the combination of high speeds, the high sulfur content of the steel, and the freezing water, the steel and the rivets became brittle and shattered upon impact with the iceberg.

LINK 3: LACK OF COMMUNICATION

It was unusually calm that evening as the ship cruised toward America, and the stillness made the icebergs even harder to see. An assigned lookout named Fred Fleet was in charge of looking for icebergs, but he had one major problem. The ship's binoculars were secured in a locker, and the only key remained on land in England, tucked into the pocket of an officer who had been replaced at the last minute.

Fleet was limited to naked-eye visibility and could only see objects that were very close to the ship. Later, the English officer's testimony revealed that had Fleet had access to the binoculars, he might have been able to divert the ship away from the iceberg in time.

LINK 4: LACK OF PROTOCOL

The wireless operators on duty on the *Titanic* were not members of the ship's crew. They were simply paid to relay personal messages to and from the passengers as a luxury service. They had no set procedures for message prioritization, and so many messages went ignored. One such message was a warning from a nearby ship, the *Californian*, which gave the precise location of the ice field. The warning never reached the captain because there was no process in place to shepherd it.

LINK 5: LACK OF TRAINING

After the ship collided with the iceberg, passengers and crew panicked. Not only was there no emergency evacuation plan, but none of the crew or officers had any training or experience operating the new type of davits used to lower the lifeboats. No drills were ever performed to train the crew or familiarize passengers about emergency procedures, so when it came time to use the lifeboats, the crew couldn't get them into the water quickly enough or, in some cases, at all.

LINK 6: UNPREPAREDNESS

Sadly, there were not nearly enough lifeboats for all of the passengers despite the fact that the ship had been designed to carry twice the number that were on board. They chose to carry the minimum number of lifeboats required by British regulations in order to keep the deck uncluttered. The emphasis was on looks and comfort—not on safety.

LINK 7: PANIC AND RUSHING

In the hurried panic, several of the lifeboats pulled away from the ship before they were full. Many of these lightly loaded boats did not return to help those frantically swimming in the frigid ocean waters. Of the

2,228 recorded passengers on board, only 705 made it into a lifeboat.

It wasn't the iceberg alone, or even the crash impact, that killed the passengers on board the *Titanic*. More than 1,500 deaths in the icy ocean were caused by a long string of actions fueled by forms of carelessness and not thinking about passenger safety that began long before the ship even left the port.

CHAPTER 2

M.O.S.T.
THE ULTIMATE STUPIDITY STOPPER

After decades of hearing people talk about accidents caused by carelessness and not thinking, I began to see a huge gap in the way we talk about and teach safety. In my experience, repeated trainings didn't seem to stick with some people, and real-life cautionary tales didn't seem to have a long-term effect. Yet smart people from all walks of life already know that carelessness and not thinking cause accidents and that following proper methods and thinking ahead keep them safe. Over time, the answer became crystal clear to me: we need to stop telling people to act differently and start training them to think differently. In 1990, I developed what some have described as a groundbreaking behavioral approach to employee safety training, designed to break the accident chain.

The M.O.S.T. system stands for **M**ethod **O**riented **S**afety **T**hinking® and the idea behind it is simple: when someone is Method Oriented, carelessness is eliminated; Safety Thinking replaces not thinking. When we train ourselves to think and behave in ways that remove carelessness and not thinking from the equation, we can finally stop saying, "I can't believe I did something so stupid."

WHY DOES M.O.S.T. WORK?

The M.O.S.T. system works because it's not a step-by-step training program or another safety manual. It's about honing your safety sense in all areas of your life and committing to a new way of thinking, at home as well as at work. M.O.S.T. helps people learn how to become safe and promotes the simple idea of doing what's right.

M.O.S.T. STARTS WITH WHAT YOU ALREADY KNOW

The M.O.S.T. system is extremely effective on and off the job because it builds on the simple truth that people already know and tell me time and time again: *accidents are caused by carelessness and not thinking.*

M.O.S.T. IS EASY TO LEARN AND EASY TO REMEMBER

Whenever I go on-site with clients that use our M.O.S.T. system, even years after the company adopted the idea, I always ask the employees, "Can you tell me what M.O.S.T. stands for?" A large majority answer correctly: Method Oriented Safety Thinking.® M.O.S.T. works well with working people because it makes sense; it's as comfortable as an old pair of glasses, and it fits like a broken-in pair of boots.

M.O.S.T. IS ABOUT MORE THAN SAFETY

Building a successful safety lifestyle is different from learning tedious safety procedures. When the M.O.S.T. system is applied at work, accident prevention isn't treated as a separate goal for the workforce. Being Method Oriented and applying Safety Thinking actually improves performance, service, production, and quality in addition to safety.

M.O.S.T. KEEPS SAFETY FRESH

Safety, beer, vegetables, and milk have one important thing in common: they have to be kept fresh. When you apply Method Oriented Safety Thinking,® safety is always on your mind. That means you become immune to the peaks and valleys of safety awareness that happen with periodic trainings. When you are constantly taking self-responsibility and applying M.O.S.T. as a way of life, stupidity has nowhere to grow.

M.O.S.T. IS ABOUT DOING WHAT'S RIGHT

My dad taught me that real character is built by doing the right thing even when nobody is watching. That philosophy strongly influenced the development of M.O.S.T. In fact, I often distill the M.O.S.T. system principles into the phrase "Doing the right thing, and doing things the right way." Famous football coach Vince Lombardi once said, "The difference between a successful person and others is not a lack of strength, not a lack of knowledge but rather a lack of will." This Lombardi truth aligns completely with the M.O.S.T. system. Making the conscious decision to do the right thing the right way takes vigilance and commitment, but it's also so simple. Just decide to do the right thing every time—following protocol, not taking shortcuts, listening to your gut—and safety naturally follows. When given the M.O.S.T. system, employees will intuitively start making safer decisions.

M.O.S.T. USES THINKING TO CHANGE BEHAVIOR

Henry Ford got it right when he said, "Whether you think you can or think you can't, you're right." Thinking matters. It makes a difference. Human thought is one of the most powerful forces in the universe, driving the actions that establish civilizations and start wars, invent languages, and destroy natural resources. On a personal level, our own thinking directly determines our own actions according to known and unknown consequences. It takes patience and persistence to retrain your thought patterns toward safety, but with practice, Safety Thinking becomes a powerful force. Using the M.O.S.T. system, we form habits that resist accident chain buildup in the first place. Imagine every safety thought as a fiber. As the fibers add up, they become stronger; bound together, they become a powerful rope of thinking that can prevent almost all accidents.

M.O.S.T. IS ALL ABOUT THE BIG PICTURE

On-the-job training can often become overly complicated and complex. Without the proper context, new processes themselves become burdensome, and we are quick to abandon the training we've received. We slip into shortcuts, bad habits, and complacency because we can't see the big safety picture. While an isolated safety lesson shows you how to do one thing the right way, M.O.S.T. is about training yourself to focus on doing all things the right way, all the time. You don't need an elaborate maze of complicated safety structures in order for M.O.S.T. to work effectively within a team or for an individual.

M.O.S.T. ENGINEERS OUT THE RISK

The workplaces and public institutions in our lives are held accountable for what we in the safety business call "engineering out the risk" in order to protect people from known links in the accident chain. A critical first step is designing operational systems to keep workers safe.

Companies require workers to wear earplugs, safety glasses, and PPE to protect their bodies from machinery; the Department of Transportation installs guardrails on highways along dangerous curves to keep cars on the road. Companies are also expected to follow standard administrative safety procedures, like changing shifts after a certain amount of time to avoid fatigue or establishing lock-out/tag-out procedures. The M.O.S.T. system creates a personal way to engineer out the risk, giving you the ability to very clearly and automatically distinguish between actions that reduce risks and those that multiply them.

M.O.S.T. STRATEGIES AND STORIES

In the coming chapters, I'll outline six easy Method Oriented Safety Thinking® strategies for breaking the accident chain or stopping it before it even starts to build. We'll explore:

LISTEN TO YOUR CLOSE CALLS
Learn to use close calls to your advantage.

FIND YOUR AWARENESS BALANCE
Explore how focus—and lack of focus—can make all the difference.

COMMUNICATE CLEARLY
What you do and say affects everyone around you; so does Method Oriented Safety Thinking®

TAKE A SLOWDOWN (NOT A SHORTCUT)
Learn the difference between an efficient time-saver and a dangerous habit.

TRAIN YOUR SAFETY AUTOPILOT
Learn how to direct your "gut feeling" to form strong habits that make safety second nature.

JUST DON'T DO IT
Discover the value of knowing what you don't know.

There's nothing difficult about practicing the ideas in this book, and none call to change your life dramatically. By simply thinking proactively and honing your sense of safety and awareness, you can start to incorporate M.O.S.T. into your daily life, at home and on the job.

M.O.S.T. Helps Smart People Stop Doing Stupid Things

Being smart doesn't mean you never take risks. However, smart people evaluate those risks and determine how to control them in the most effective ways. That's where the M.O.S.T. system comes in.

Smart people are Method Oriented.
They do things the right and safe way—every time. They buckle their seatbelts—every single time. They don't use their cell phones or text while driving—every single time. They follow safe procedures—every single time.

Smart people use Safety Thinking.
They can take risks and be adventurous and even daring. However, they consciously think about their surroundings and weigh the possible consequences of their adventures and then use that thinking to guide their behaviors and actions in order to manage risk.

CHAPTER 3

LISTEN TO YOUR CLOSE CALLS

We've established that accidents don't just happen, but unfortunately, they do happen. And they rarely come out of the blue. Most of the time, we actually have an opportunity to preview the accident (and possibly change the future) through the near misses and close calls that sometimes come first.

We all experience close calls, like sending just one text message in traffic and looking up just in time to slam on the brake to avoid hitting the car in front of you, or catching your balance at the last minute as you stand on an unsteady rolling chair to reach a box on a high shelf. And for some of us, close calls on the job can mean nearly losing a limb or even your life operating heavy machinery without following safety protocol. Like full-blown accidents, close calls happen when carelessness and/or not thinking are in play.

Close calls can be dangerous even when nothing bad happens. In fact, the near misses and bullet-dodgers that leave us feeling the luckiest are perhaps the most dangerous close calls of all because they allow us to believe that it's possible to do whatever stupid thing we were doing without suffering a major consequence (this time).

Close calls trick smart people into one of the most destructive forms of stupidity: the repeated kind. We're lured by our luck into a particular brand of denial—a risky complacency and a feeling of being "bulletproof" that leads to bad habits and, eventually, causes completely preventable accidents.

How many times have you said to yourself, "It was only a matter of time," when the damaged tool you're using finally leads to a serious cut on your finger, when your shortcut fails, or when a risky behavior finally ends in disaster, be it large or small? That's how close calls work—they evolve into the kind of accidents you could see coming a mile away, leaving you to shake your head and say, "How could I have done something so stupid?"

THE ONE-ARMED FARMER

I'm a firm believer in the old adage, "If you take your boy hunting, you won't have to go hunting for your boy." I've taken my son Joey on countless hunting trips over the years that presented hundreds of teaching moments. Even now, the lesson from this story is the one he remembers best, and it didn't even come from me.

Joey was thirteen at the time, and we'd gone to Montana together to go elk and deer hunting. It was a full week of tent camping, freezing temperatures, and a very successful hunt. Joey killed the largest mule deer ever taken on the ranch where we were camping, and I didn't do so badly myself—after just three days, we'd both hit the maximum number of deer our hunting tags would permit. We still had four days to experience the beauty of the Montana wilderness and explore our surroundings.

News spread about Joey's impressive deer, and one of the neighboring farmers came by to check out the rack of antlers and invite us to his farm. Over the next few days, we spent quite a bit of time with Brian. We rode in his pickup truck across the thousands of acres that he farmed, talking and taking in the incredible scenery. Brian was the third generation to farm the land, running thousands of cattle and harvesting many tons of wheat every year. As a curious youngster, Joey had endless questions about farm life that Brian was happy to answer. Brian showed a genuine interest in my safety-consulting business as well and seemed to have more of a personal connection to the subject than most. He had initially introduced himself to us as "the One-Armed Farmer" due to what I had assumed was a tragic farming accident.

On our last day in Montana, we'd been out on Brian's farm all day exploring the land and soaking up the last bit of our time out West. We ended up back in one of his barns, where he showed us some of the biggest John Deere tractors and combines I'd ever seen. As we admired the massive machinery, Brian said, "If you think these things are impressive, come around back. There's an old hay baler I want to show you—one of the first ever made."

We rounded the corner expecting to admire a piece of restored vintage farm equipment, but Brian continued, "You guys have been awfully respectful not asking about my arm. I thought you might want to see this hunk of junk, considering all the accident stories you've told me. Maybe you can use my story too." He patted the rusting old baler. "This is the beast that took my arm."

"I know I'm definitely not the first farmer this has happened to," he continued. "Plenty of us have lost fingers, arms, legs, and sometimes even lives around equipment like this. But I'm here to tell you it's not because the equipment is so dangerous. It's because of the stupid things we do, even when we know better."

Brian walked around the old round baler in the clear Montana light. "Most of the time, we get lucky," he said, looking back toward the house. "A friend of mine just last year got the cuff of his pants caught on a bolt as he stepped over a grain auger that was attached to his tractor, and the fabric got caught up in the drive shaft. That auger ripped his pants clean off in a split second while he just stood there, and he had to walk back to the house shivering in his skivvies!"

At thirteen, Joey found that one pretty hilarious. Brian smiled and laughed a little himself.

"It sounds funny now, and he was pretty embarrassed," Brian said, "but also unbelievably lucky. If his pants hadn't been so old and threadbare they wouldn't have ripped so easily, and it would have been his whole body twisted around that drive shaft, starting with his leg. Sadly, it happens like that too often."

He patted the baler again and paused for a minute. "Over the years,

I lost three gloves in that baler before it got me."

"We haven't used it since my accident, more than thirty-three years ago. We bought it used at an equipment auction, and it never worked quite right. It would pull the fresh cut hay in, but the intake chute kept clogging up, and I'd have to stop and clear out the bunches of hay to get things moving again. At first, I was really careful to put the tractor in park and kill the power to the baler before I got close to it. But man, it just happened so often and was such a pain in the neck, at some point I just started putting the tractor in park and jumping down without stopping to kill the power to the baler."

Joey winced and his eyes darted to the place where Brian's arm should have been. He understood where the story was going.

"The first time it happened, my glove got pulled in so fast that it took me a minute to even figure out what was going on. It freaked me out so bad that I went right back to doing everything right when I had to unclog it. You could say I was scared straight for years after that. But over time I just slipped back into my old ways, and after the second and then the third glove... I guess I thought I was either lucky or bulletproof, but I wasn't either one. I just kept sticking my hand up there with the baler running all the time like it was no big deal."

EVERY CLOSE CALL IS A POWERFUL WARNING INTENDED TO ALERT US TO DANGEROUS RISKS AND STEER US IN ANOTHER DIRECTION.

"Sure enough, eventually it was my hand that got caught in the belts that roll up the hay. That old baler got more than my glove that time. It tore my whole right arm off of my body in a matter of seconds. I panicked and went into shock for who knows how long and then somehow got ahold of myself enough to realize I was going to die if I didn't make it back to the house to get help. I was about a mile away in one of the back fields, luckily not far considering how much land we work out here. That ride back to the house was the longest tractor ride of my life. My arm was so mangled up, I don't even remember the pain, just a voice telling me that my life was on the line, and I needed to get home as fast as possible. Later the doctors told me the nerves were so scrambled, it saved me from the full force of the pain, and if it had been a clean cut I'd have bled to death in the field. I have five kids. I still wrestle with how close I came to leaving them."

Brian turned and started back toward the barn and the shiny new equipment inside. Joey and I followed in silence, not sure what to say. Brian turned and put his big hand on Joey's shoulder and looked him in the eye.

"Son, I spent a lot of years beating myself up over how one careless mistake cost me my arm, and almost my life. But looking back now, I know it's really a miracle it didn't happen to me sooner. I never should have taken a stupid shortcut even once, let alone hundreds of times. You'd think one glove would have been enough to make me come to my senses."

CLOSE CALLS: OPPORTUNITIES IN DISGUISE

Close calls are not the same thing as stupidity, and having close calls does not make you a stupid person. We all have near-miss experiences that can be scary, miraculous, painful, funny, or all of the above. Close calls stop us in our tracks, at least for the moment. But more often than not, we just shake our heads in amazement or catch our breath afterward and then go on with our lives.

I believe those close calls are more than the embarrassing flubs or lucky breaks we take them for. Every close call is a powerful warning intended to alert us to dangerous risks and steer us in another direction. It's when we ignore them or even allow the same close calls to happen again and again—like the farmer's first three gloves—that we allow carelessness and not thinking to grow into stupidity.

I'm sure we can all think of situations that could have been worse: a broken ankle that could easily have been a lost leg; a strained back that could have been a life-threatening injury; a fender bender that could have been a fatal head-on collision. It's easy to speculate on how dramatic the consequences could have been as a way of thanking our lucky stars, but that sense of grateful relief alone doesn't serve us well in the future.

You have the power to make every close call into more than just a taste of future disaster. Every close call signals the potential buildup of an accident chain and helps us pinpoint the place where we can shift our routine or behavior to break it. Every time we brush up against danger thanks to our own carelessness or not thinking, we have the opportunity to answer the close call with a conscious change in how we act.

ANSWERING CLOSE CALLS

Regardless of whether we walk away from a close call unscathed or with some battle scars to show, the way we behave after an accident or close call is what's most important. Answering a close call by changing the way we think and act is one of the simplest and most direct ways to stop stupidity.

We have a choice to make every time we get lucky, whether we've just lost a glove to an old piece of farm equipment or narrowly avoided a collision due to distracted driving. We can either avoid future disaster by breaking the accident chain with our behavior, starting now, or continue to practice stupidity, letting close calls pile up until a future accident forces us to change our behavior down the road, and probably not in the way we'd choose. Like the One-Armed Farmer, we can choose to listen or push our luck. Which do you think he'd choose in hindsight?

STUPIDITY STOPPER

LISTEN TO YOUR CLOSE CALLS

➡ Close calls are accident previews.

➡ Close calls trick us into repeated stupidity because we feel lucky at first and eventually feel bulletproof.

➡ Close calls signal the buildup of an accident chain.

SMART MOVE **Break the Accident Chain**

HOW YOU BEHAVE AFTER THE CLOSE CALL IS MORE IMPORTANT THAN WHAT YOU DID TO CAUSE IT. CHANGING THE WAY WE THINK AND ACT IS ONE OF THE SIMPLEST AND MOST DIRECT WAYS TO STOP STUPIDITY.

➡ Train yourself to listen to your close calls; every one is a powerful warning.

➡ A close call is your chance to pinpoint the place where you can change behavior or shift routine to break the accident chain.

➡ Treat close calls like gold.

CHAPTER 4

FIND YOUR AWARENESS BALANCE

We've all heard expressions like "Look before you leap!" and "Keep your eye on the ball!" They're familiar reminders to pay attention to our surroundings in order to avoid disaster, failure, injury, and—let's face it—stupidity. Whether we're in the car, on the job, or at home, our surroundings constantly present new risks, challenges, and opportunities. We choose with our thinking and behavior whether to pay attention or ignore them.

In all of my years leading safety training classes, I've asked nearly every group of employees the same question: "Who in this room has never missed a day of work because of an accident?" I'll typically get a few hands raised proudly in the air; some will boast that they've been accident-free for several decades. I do it not only to give them a little much-deserved recognition but because I believe these people are powerful examples of Safety Thinking on the job. When I ask them to share their safety secrets with the rest of the group, I overwhelmingly hear the same thing time and time again: "Be aware of your surroundings."

It sounds so easy, right? Just pay attention. Look around. What could be simpler? In this day and age of multitasking and 24/7 connectivity, constant demands are being made on our attention. From the ping of a phone signaling a text to a digital billboard that changes its message as we drive by, we're bombarded with sights, sounds, and tasks that demand our time right now.

It's an amazing age to be alive. New technology makes it possible for one person to do a job that used to require several people; we're quickly able to accomplish tasks that were unfathomable fifty or even twenty years ago. Unfortunately, we haven't evolved as quickly as our demands assume. Our lives encourage (and require!) that we give our attention and awareness so many places that we're out of practice at giving anything 100 percent of our focus. We get so consumed by the task(s) at hand that we lose sight of the world around us, and our attention scatters like the proverbial herd of cats.

AWARENESS GIVES YOU CONTROL OVER YOUR SURROUNDINGS AND, MORE SPECIFICALLY, CONTROL OVER A POTENTIALLY DEVELOPING ACCIDENT CHAIN.

Your own awareness of your environment can be your most powerful safety tool, and that's a dangerous thing to sacrifice in the name of productivity. Awareness gives you control over your surroundings and, more specifically, control over a potentially developing accident chain. Think the driver in the car next to you is swerving? Move over, and let him pass. Don't like the way that heavy box is teetering toward your head from the tallest shelf? You have the power to get out of the way, but only if you notice what's happening around you.

Awareness keeps risk in check. It puts you squarely in the "now," allowing you to make better, faster, more-informed decisions on the spot that can dramatically impact your safety, your life, and the lives of others. Awareness overrides carelessness and not thinking, which helps you eliminate stupidity.

As a father and grandfather now, I can only imagine the feeling in my dad's gut when carelessness and not thinking collided in our backyard when I was a kid.

Dad was the type that loved the challenge of a tough project, and I loved the feeling of sharing his work ethic. One summer day as a young kid, I was helping him cut an overgrown patch of privet hedge in our side yard. I stood there, barefoot and shirtless, picking up the discarded branches and vines and throwing them in a nearby ditch. It was a job I'd taken on myself, without announcing my presence. I worked behind him proudly for several minutes, waiting for him to acknowledge my vital contributions to the cause.

We didn't own pruning shears, so Dad used an old handsaw, swinging it like a machete to hack away at the smaller branches and get to the larger branches and vines. He had no idea I was standing right behind him picking up the fallen branches as he continued to swing away in the afternoon heat.

You can probably guess what came next. As I ran toward my dad to pick up a fallen branch, the cutting edge of the saw hit me right across the face. It came down fast, and the sharp teeth dug into the flesh right above my eye, knocking me to the ground. As serious cuts on the head tend to do, it bled profusely. Dad grabbed me right away, carried me to the car, and headed straight to the emergency room.

I was aware of my surroundings—I saw Dad swinging the handsaw—but I was too young to understand that I was in harm's way. I can't even imagine what my extremely safety-conscious father must have felt as he drove me to the hospital. I ended up with stitches, but I think my dad was more scarred by the incident than I was. I know he must have kicked himself for years over the fact that he acted carelessly, not paying attention to his surroundings as he was swinging the saw in an admittedly dangerous way. Needless to say, I walked away having learned my own safety lesson because of the experience.

As a young child driven by the passion to be involved with my dad, this was not stupidity. But it served me well as a parent and now a grandparent to be super aware of my surroundings at all times, especially when children are present.

READING THE RED FLAGS

Put simply, awareness is about noticing the world around us and seeing it through the lens of accident prevention. Like the close calls in the previous chapter, awareness alerts us to valuable warnings and red flags that can help us change our routine, modify our surroundings, or adjust what we're doing. And also like close calls, willingly ignoring our surroundings—and the warnings they contain—leads to dangerous situations.

Awareness can mean anticipating and scanning for what could happen next. Visualizing cause and effect allows us to take proper precautions for whatever might come at us: injury, damage, or setbacks that cost us time on the job. Being aware of icy road conditions leads us to visualize sliding across lanes of traffic, prompting us to drive slowly and more cautiously; being aware that the power is on keeps an electrician from electrocuting himself on a jobsite.

Awareness can also mean simply taking stock of your surroundings, like knowing where the exits are in a crowded restaurant, knowing where to find an eyewash station on a jobsite, or remembering which exit you just passed on the highway should you need to call for help. Years ago on a crowded flight, I took my seat next to a man and thought I'd woken him from a cat nap. I apologized, and he told me he wasn't sleeping; he always closed his eyes before a flight and visualized walking to the two nearest exits, calling this his "emergency mind mapping" strategy. When you're aware of your surroundings in the event of an accident, you can react in an informed way.

A lack of awareness can lead us either to distraction or tunnel vision, two states of mind on complete opposite ends of the spectrum.

DISTRACTION

We're expected to multitask more and more in our lives, and we sometimes even brag about it or wear our multitasking as a badge of honor. Unfortunately, multitasking is a myth. We're not actually focusing on all those irons in the fire. We're just getting more adept at shifting from one to the next and back again.

When we take our focus off of one thing, we lose control over our place in that particular environment. When we practice staying in the moment instead of staying in multiple moments, our controls are stable, and the likeliness of an accident is greatly reduced.

One of my son's friends told me this story several years ago when he traveled with our family on spring break. As a soon-to-be high school senior, Drew had been given several responsibilities in addition to his summer job; one of those was to drive his younger siblings to and from their various day camps and commitments while his parents were at work. One sunny morning, he had just dropped his brother at a friend's house and was driving his little sister to her dance class, trying to make it on time to his own shift at a local restaurant. Drew was a self-described cautious driver. He wasn't in the habit of speeding, didn't listen to loud music, and he almost always observed his parents' "no phones, no exceptions" rule while driving. He was especially careful with his little brother and sister in the car.

> **WHEN YOU'RE AWARE OF YOUR SURROUNDINGS IN THE EVENT OF AN ACCIDENT, YOU CAN REACT IN AN INFORMED WAY.**

Drew and his sister cruised down their country road toward town, with the sun coming up high behind them. They were in a line of several cars and directly behind a neighbor's farm truck that was piled high with branches and other debris from a recent storm. Drew's phone rang as they took a semi-sharp curve, and he saw that it was his mother, checking in. Knowing she'd worry if he didn't answer, he made the decision to answer the call. Sure enough, she was just making sure everyone was getting where they needed to go on time.

The next thing Drew knew, his car slammed into the truck in front of him, and he was pinned to the seat by his own steering wheel. He couldn't reach his sister. He described it as the most terrifying moment of his young life.

Drew never saw the brake lights on the neighbor's truck, as they were covered in mud; the sun was blinding in the rearview mirror, and he didn't see the car in front of the farm truck make a sudden turn. Drew had no control over most of the links in this accident chain, but his decision to answer the phone despite his "no exceptions" rule had certainly divided his attention between the road and the conversation. Because he was talking to his mother, he didn't see what was about to happen; in fact, he added his own link to a growing accident chain.

The car was totaled, but Drew and his sister were miraculously fine, save for a few bumps and bruises. Drew still wonders if he could have avoided disaster by ignoring the ringing distraction, and his mother still kicks herself for calling when she knew he'd be driving. Those small decisions still haunt both of them today.

As of this writing, nearly a quarter of all auto accidents in the US involve the use of cell phones; more specifically, people trying to shift between the app or conversation in their hands and the task of driving. Even a few seconds' loss of focus can be deadly when you're traveling at sixty or even thirty miles per hour.

Sometimes distractions come from within. Simple daydreaming or "checking out" can be dangerous and lead to some scary close calls, but some of the most dangerous forms of distraction are our own physical states that keep us from being aware of our surroundings.

Take fatigue, for example. When we allow ourselves to get too tired, our awareness batteries drain, and we're unable to focus very well. We no longer notice potential pitfalls, and our reaction time slows considerably. We hear about this all the time with single-vehicle tractor-trailer accidents—drivers spend long hours behind the wheel and get extremely sleepy. They lose their focus, running off the road, sometimes to fatal consequences. When drivers learn to see fatigue as a dangerous distraction that robs them of their safety awareness, they can take steps to eliminate it by pulling over to sleep, stretch their legs, or get a cup of coffee.

TUNNEL VISION

On the other end of the awareness spectrum, we have the incredible phenomenon of tunnel vision. While distraction is about letting our focus stray from the task at hand, tunnel vision is what happens when frustration, stress, and pressure essentially erase our surroundings altogether.

Take the example of my neighbor, an experienced driver who had never tackled the task of driving in reverse with a small utility trailer attached to his truck. Backing into the driveway seemed simple, but it wasn't. Each try got worse instead of better. He became agitated (and perhaps embarrassed) as the trailer jackknifed to the side over and over, eventually ramming into the side of the garage. It was as if he didn't even see the building. His intense focus and frustration over straightening out the trailer had eclipsed his awareness of his surroundings.

But wait, didn't we just say that focus is a good thing? Shouldn't we try to be "in the zone?"

My good friend Bob Cummins worked as an NFL assistant coach for the New Orleans Saints and the Cleveland Browns. Bob is now in his nineties and sits with his dear wife Emmy in the pew behind my wife and I at church every Sunday. Bob and I have had many conversations over the years about "seeing" our surroundings; one of my favorite stories involves the man he describes as the master of being in the zone. Blanton Collier was the head coach of the Cleveland Browns in 1964 and responsible for leading the team to a NFL Championship win. According to my friend Bob, Coach Collier would talk with players for hours about the importance of being able to intensely focus. He trained quarterbacks not just

TUNNEL VISION IS WHAT HAPPENS WHEN FRUSTRATION, STRESS, AND PRESSURE ESSENTIALLY ERASE OUR SURROUNDINGS ALTOGETHER.

to look at the receiver but to try to look so hard that they could see the threads on the receiver's jersey between the printed numbers; he trained receivers in the art of focus until they could look at an airborne football and actually see the small raised dots on the ball. That's what it means to be in the zone. It's a hyper-focus so intense that it helps move the entire body into an unconscious level of peak performance. When champions move into the zone, time seems to slow down, the body and mind work in precise harmony, and performance soars. It's a beautiful thing.

So what's the difference between being in the zone and tunnel vision, besides the fact that one wins championships and one leads to thousands of dollars in garage repairs? The key word is control. When we're in the zone, we're exercising a powerful laser focus that intensifies our awareness and control over mind and body in order to execute a task with precision. When we are in the zone, the unconscious mind takes over and our world slows down, allowing us to achieve maximum control. When we're experiencing tunnel vision, on the other hand, we're not in control at all. Tunnel vision is the opposite of being in the zone. It's a dangerous type of focus that happens when we lose awareness of our surroundings and, therefore, also lose control of our thinking and behavior.

A few years ago, I was shopping in a sporting goods store and got into a conversation with an employee who was a former cop. We'll call him Josh. He said he'd had enough of being a policeman and decided his life was more important than to put it at risk on a daily basis.

Josh told me that in his six years as a police officer, he'd had only one serious close call. He had responded to a domestic dispute at a private residence. As he stepped out of the patrol car, a man appeared on the front porch of the house and yelled for him to leave. Josh crouched down behind his car and watched the man run toward him with a shotgun, screaming obscenities and demanding that Josh get off of his property. When the man reached the end of the driveway, he started firing. The bullets hit the side of the patrol car.

Josh said he had never been so scared in his life. He pointed his weapon at the man and warned him to drop the shotgun. Instead of complying, the man fired again and started running toward the police car. In absolute fear for his life, Josh began firing, hitting the man once.

As he frantically radioed for help, Josh reported that he'd fired four times. When his partner arrived, he discovered that he had actually fired fourteen times, not four. The fear of losing his life had caused his vision and everything around him to narrow dramatically, and he lost sight of how many times he'd fired his gun.

We can all think of times when we've had tunnel vision: racing to get to work on time and blowing through a stop sign because we "just didn't see it," or working so intensely to put together a piece of furniture that we realize we've connected everything upside down. For Josh and others who put themselves in high-stress, life-or-death situations regularly, the loss of perspective is a real danger.

One of the most tragic and preventable plane crash stories I know is the story of Eastern Airlines flight 401, a tragic incident where an entire crew suffered from a sort of collective tunnel vision that resulted in a fatal 1972 crash. In their effort to frantically solve a problem with the landing gear, no one noticed that the autopilot had accidentally become disengaged. Without the autopilot holding altitude, the plane gradually started falling from 2,000 feet, crashing into the swampy Florida Everglades below. The crew had become so focused on fixing a mechanical failure that they failed to remember their number one priority: flying the plane.

FINDING THE "AWARENESS BALANCE"

The key to staying aware of your surroundings is finding your own sweet spot between distraction and tunnel vision. When we find that focus and train ourselves to stay in that mental space, we break the accident chain by engineering out the risks of distraction and tunnel vision as we go along.

So how do we find that balance? When I was working toward getting my pilot's license, we learned about something called "conscious cross-checking," and the concept has become an important part of my safety trainings as well. For an airplane pilot, there are so many gauges and dials and instruments to check; focusing on just one thing erases the big picture (as it did on flight 401), and shifting focus away from the instrument panel for any reason can easily result in disaster.

Cross-checking simply means maintaining an ongoing awareness of the flight environment with a smooth scanning of the area. Over time, it becomes second nature.

When we practice conscious cross-checking in everyday life, we're constantly taking stock of our surroundings, thinking one step ahead of the present, and anticipating change in order to react appropriately.

THE KEY TO STAYING AWARE OF YOUR SURROUNDINGS IS FINDING YOUR OWN SWEET SPOT BETWEEN DISTRACTION AND TUNNEL VISION.

Just as a driver looks at the road far ahead instead of at the steering wheel, staying "ahead of forward motion" is essential to staying in control.

Think of a mother with two young children walking through a busy grocery store parking lot. She's constantly checking to make sure both children are nearby, scanning for moving vehicles and cars in reverse, and moving forward toward her own car. She's doing a lot of work in that moment, but it's not multi-tasking. She's not hopping from one thing to the next while ignoring the other pieces of the puzzle. Her awareness is singular, but it covers a lot of ground thanks to cross-checking.

I once heard an old pilot say, "I wear suspenders plus a belt just for good measure." Of course, as a safety professional, that saying gives me a chuckle. Having a backup system is important, whether you're flying a plane, staying safe on the job, or just trying to keep your pants up. The good news is that you have a backup system already installed, if you just choose to engage it. Your conscious awareness and sense of your surroundings protect against danger in the same way, kicking into gear at the first sign of disturbance. When accidents happen—and we know they will—being aware of your surroundings allows your reactions to be quicker, smarter, and safer.

FIND YOUR AWARENESS BALANCE

➡ We're expected to give our attention and awareness to so many places that we can't give anything 100 percent of our focus.

➡ Multitasking is a myth. It's really just about shifting our focus from one thing to the next and back again.

➡ A lack of awareness can lead us to opposite ends of the spectrum:
   - **DISTRACTION:** letting our focus stray from the task at hand
   - **TUNNEL VISION:** fixation on one aspect of a situation rather than the task at hand

SMART MOVE ❭ Break the Accident Chain

AWARENESS OF YOUR SURROUNDINGS CAN OVERRIDE CARELESSNESS AND NOT THINKING, ELIMINATING STUPIDITY WHEN IT MATTERS MOST.

➡ Learn to use your awareness of your environment as your most powerful safety tool.

➡ Stay aware of your surroundings by finding your own sweet spot between distraction and tunnel vision.

➡ Practice Conscious Cross Checking:
   - Constantly take stock of your surroundings.
   - Think one step ahead of the present.
   - Anticipate change in order to react appropriately.

CHAPTER 5

COMMUNICATE CLEARLY

Being aware of your surroundings also means being aware of the people around you. Where are they standing, what are they doing, and what are they about to do? What information do they need from you to be able to stay safe, and what do you need to know from them to keep yourself out of harm's way? How might they be affected by what you're doing or are about to do?

We've all been in situations where we've encountered what we call a "well-oiled machine": seven line cooks seamlessly prepping a never-ending line of individual orders, for example, or a team of skilled ER doctors and nurses treating a patient together when every second counts. They seem to know each other's next move before it happens, and they can execute complex maneuvers in concert without exchanging a single word. We know this phenomenon as teamwork at its best, and none of it would be possible without practiced, conscious communication.

In high-risk jobs especially, communication between workers makes the difference between an accident that is allowed to happen and a zero-injury environment—sometimes between life and death. Electric linemen know this better than most. Working on top of a utility pole with 50,000 volts of electricity, they must maintain constant, clear communication with all members of the team on the ground and even on different poles, many times under extremely stressful weather conditions. One mistake or misunderstanding can be life-changing (or life-ending) for several workers in just an instant. There's a reason they say that "linemen don't need erasers on their pencils." There's just no room for error in their world. Whether it's a distinctive hand signal from the top of one pole to another or a specific verbal cue from the ground up, communication must be exactly right the first time, every time.

In those situations and many others, each person on the team not only understands his or her role in the big-picture result, but he or she also understands how to give and receive information quickly and clearly—even if it's nonverbally—in order to work toward a shared goal. We can see safety as a grand exercise in teamwork too. Whether on the job or in everyday life, picture yourself as a member of a massive safety team. What kinds of communication do you need to practice in order to exchange important information with others around you? How can you play your part in the big picture of keeping yourself and everyone around you safe?

Safety communication extends far beyond the words we say. Hand signals can stop an entire line of traffic; the flip of a switch activates police lights and sirens; setting out a "wet floor" pylon alerts customers to a potential danger.

Without safe communication, even the office break room can be just as dangerous as the factory floor. I once interviewed a woman named Marjorie, a project manager at a large advertising agency, who suffered a serious injury in the employee kitchen doing something few people think of as risky: using the ice and water dispenser built into the refrigerator door. As Marjorie stepped toward the fridge after lunch to fill her empty water bottle, she slipped on a small puddle, lost her balance, and hit the floor hard. Her right elbow caught most of her weight, and Marjorie felt an immediate searing pain shoot through the elbow and down her arm. The elbow was shattered, and Marjorie was rushed to the ER, where she was in surgery within hours. Her recovery time was difficult, and she was unable to work for an extended period of time. The incident resulted in dramatic physical and economic hardship for Marjorie and a significant personnel loss during Marjorie's recovery that impacted the entire office.

While I was investigating the claim, several of Marjorie's coworkers told me that they knew the ice dispenser kicked out an extra ice cube or two from time to time when people used it, but not one of them had notified a supervisor or maintenance person to have the problem fixed. It was a classic case of carelessness feeding stupidity: instead of taking just a few minutes to communicate for safety's sake, they allowed a known risk to become Marjorie's very real problem.

Marjorie's story reminds me of the "Body Story," a timeless illustration of responsibility by an unknown author that has circulated everywhere from the boardroom to the classroom:

This is a story about four people named Everybody, Somebody, Anybody, and Nobody.

There was an important job to be done and Everybody was sure that Somebody would do it.

Anybody could have done it, but Nobody did it.

Somebody got angry about that because it was Everybody's job.

Everybody thought Anybody could do it, but Nobody realized that Everybody wouldn't do it.

It ended up that Everybody blamed Somebody when Nobody did what Anybody could have done!

—Author Unknown

Like in the Body Story, communication is one area where the link between carelessness and not thinking is perhaps most direct and tangible. When we're careless with communication, we're not taking the time or making the effort delivering or receiving the information we need to prevent an accident. And by failing to communicate, we often are directly responsible for someone else's not thinking.

In the early 1990s, I investigated an accident at a small nursing home in rural Florida. I met with a certified nursing assistant named Misty, who started our interview by tearfully telling me she'd always wanted to become a nurse. Her mom worked as a registered nurse, and Misty was inspired by her dedication and desire to serve others. Misty was working toward earning a BSN degree and had taken the CNA position just a few months before to start gaining some hands-on experience as she worked to pay for school. Her supervisor told me that Misty had been through an in-depth orientation and observation period and was considered to be a fast learner and one of the nursing home's brightest and most caring clinical employees.

On the day of the accident, Misty was responding to one of her favorite patients, Doris, who had pressed her call button after falling to the floor. Misty found Doris wedged in a tight space between the bed and the wall and immediately called for help from a fellow new hire. She knew the lift would be difficult due to Doris's weight and the tight space, but she was anxious and eager to help.

Recalling her orientation training, Misty counted to three before lifting, assuming that her partner was also readying herself to assist with the lift. Unfortunately, Misty didn't say anything about lifting before she started counting; she didn't make eye contact or check in with her partner at all. If she had, she would have seen that the other CNA was still struggling to attach the gait belt around Doris's waist for support. Not only did she not connect verbally with her teammate, but Misty also didn't tell the patient on the floor that on "three" she should be prepared to move to a standing position.

To a fly on the wall, it would appear that Misty just counted to three out of the blue and tried to lift a 200-pound patient on her own. Misty started to lift without the help of her coworker, and Doris grabbed her around the neck, jerking her down on her knees. Misty felt an explosion of pain in her lower back—after all, she'd just tried to lift 200 pounds of weight alone.

An MRI at the emergency room showed a severely herniated disc, requiring immediate surgery. Misty thought she was communicating before the accident, but without first making a connection with her partner and with the patient, she was simply talking, not connecting. Her plan to care for others was sidelined by a need to stop everything—

school, work, and more—to tend to her own health.

Communication breakdowns can be caused by a misunderstanding, like in Misty's case, driven by not thinking. It can also be a dangerous product of carelessness when we fail to communicate information fully or at all, even when we see an accident chain forming. When I attended the 2015 Tennessee Safety Congress, the OSHA state director took the stage to deliver a powerful message. He simply read the names of the twenty-nine people who had lost their lives in industrial accidents so far that year and asked the audience to stand and observe a thirty-second moment of silence in their memory. It was a truly impactful moment for everyone in the room.

Once the crowd was seated again, the director said that his compliance officers had completed investigations on every fatal accident and had concluded that every death could have been prevented if someone would have had the courage to stand up and simply say, "Stop."

How many times in your own life has this been true? If someone had stopped to question a risky financial decision, an unhealthy personal relationship, or an unsafe physical situation, what pitfalls and consequences could you have avoided? How could you have helped someone break his or her own accident chain?

NO MATTER HOW WELL QUALIFIED, EXPERIENCED, OR PROFESSIONAL YOU ARE, AS LONG AS HUMAN BEINGS ARE INVOLVED, ACCIDENTS CAN ALWAYS HAPPEN.

Sadly, one of the of the most tragic losses in aviation history could have been prevented with a simple "stop." In March 1977, a bomb exploded at Gran Canaria Airport in Spain's Canary Islands, temporarily diverting all flights to nearby Los Rodeos Tenerife Airport. Nearly 600 innocent people died that day, but not because of the bomb. They died on two perfectly safe Boeing 747 Jumbo Jets using the only runway at Los Rodeos.

As a small regional airport, Los Rodeos had only one runway and one main taxiway; it was never designed to handle the five diverted airliners that quickly overwhelmed the limited staff. The controllers on duty decided to have the planes park temporarily on the main taxiway just as low, thick fog clouds began rolling in across the mountains. With no ground radar and almost zero visibility, the controllers had no way of knowing where the aircraft were yet still had to prepare anxious crews and passengers for departure before more planes joined the overcrowded runway.

WE'RE RARELY IN CONTROL OF ALL THE CIRCUMSTANCES THAT SURROUND US, BUT WE CAN BE IN CONTROL OF THE WAY WE COMMUNICATE.

A Pan Am flight was ready to depart from Los Rodeos but was blocked by a KLM aircraft waiting on fuel. When the KLM was finally fueled, the tower instructed it to approach the end of the runway and turn around to prepare for takeoff. The controller cleared the Pan Am to follow and then take the third exit on the left to clear the runway for the KLM's departure.

As both planes began to move, a dense cloud of fog rolled across the runway, making visibility nearly impossible. The runway center lights were not working, and the Pan Am crew slowed the plane to a crawl, looking desperately for the poorly marked exits. All the while, the nearby KLM was anxious to depart and radioed the tower to report that they were "at takeoff." The tower responded with "OK... stand by for takeoff. I will call you." An investigation later showed that the only part the KLM pilot heard was "OK." The rest was garbled due to radio static. The KLM crew raised questions among themselves about the position of the unseen Pan Am aircraft, but no one said, "Stop. Something is not right here." The pilot began takeoff.

By the time the KLM pilot saw the Pan Am aircraft on the runway in front of him, it was too late to engage the brakes. He tried to execute a premature liftoff to go over the plane, but the maneuver failed, and the KLM jet crashed into the top of the taxiing Pan Am jet. Both aircraft erupted in flames.

Only fifty-six passengers and five crew members on the Pan Am survived, while all 234 passengers and fourteen crew members aboard the KLM aircraft perished.

Many years after the tragic loss of 583 lives at the Los Rodeos Airport, a retired investigator summed up what he'd learned from the investigation: no matter how well qualified, experienced, or professional you are, as long as human beings are involved, accidents can always happen. Unfortunately, poor communication is often the reason.

FINDING A SAFETY LANGUAGE

We're rarely in control of all the circumstances that surround us, but we can be in control of the way we communicate. The aviation industry learned from the incident in the Canary Islands that it was vital to maintain a constant safety touchstone with a common language to eliminate miscommunication and avoid disaster.

In aviation communications today, the word "takeoff" is now reserved only in reference to "cleared for takeoff." When an aircraft is instructed to position itself on an active runway in preparation for departure, the instructions are "Line UP and WAIT." The pilot is never authorized to start the departure roll until the tower controller identifies the aircraft and says, "Cleared for takeoff." This common safety language could have saved all 583 lives that day in 1977, and it undoubtedly has saved an untold number of lives since.

The healthcare industry is another area where there is simply no room for error, and it is a great example of a working safety language. With so many people contributing to patient care in an ever-changing set of circumstances, constant, clear communication is absolutely vital. But how do you transfer volumes of minute-to-minute information over multiple shift changes, interdepartmental referrals, and so on?

Once again, you engineer out the risk wherever possible with a simple, common safety language understood by all staff members. At almost every hospital in the country, patients verify their names with each new staff encounter to double-check against their name bracelets; the staff members know this is the fastest and clearest way to confirm they're looking at the right record. When my wife recently had knee surgery to repair a meniscus tear in her right knee, a nurse wrote the words "right knee" with an ink pen just above the knee. When the doctor came in, she used a permanent marker to mark where the incisions would be. Then, both the nurse and doctor confirmed separately with my wife which knee was to have surgery. To the patient, communication measures like these might seem repetitive, overly simplistic, or even strange. However, to a hospital, they're vital steps in clear communication and accident prevention.

I use a common safety language with my young grandkids all the time. When we're out on a walk or are out playing in the park, we're often surrounded by the constant sounds of voices, laughter, and noises coming from all directions. I know from experience that in this environment, every parent and grandparent voice starts to sound the same; so does every child's. It's easy for kids to get overwhelmed by all the sensory input, and hearing a command like "Stop!" can mean about a hundred different things in that one moment: "Stop picking your nose," "Stop teasing your sister," "Stop running up the slide backward," or something far more serious, like "Stop! You're about to run out in front of a speeding car." In a world where they hear "stop" constantly (and become somewhat desensitized to it), how can we be sure they know exactly what we mean when it really counts? My wife and I have clearly established with them that "stop" means "stop doing X, Y, or Z," but when we shout "RED LIGHT," they physically stop in their tracks. Whether that's at a sidewalk curb, at the edge of the playground, or just before they climb into the grizzly bear pen at the zoo, red light means something instant and specific, and it works. They might still be picking their noses when they screech to a halt, but they stop moving away from us when we need to keep them safe.

We've also trained them that if we get separated in a crowd, they're to shout for Ron and Carol, not Grandma and Grandpa. In a loud environment full of joyful families, it would be so easy to not hear the panicked voice of one of our own little ones. But because we have a special safety language, they have the power to get our attention faster when it matters most.

SPEAKING THE SAME LANGUAGE

What about Misty though? She was using the safety language of her job, but she got hurt anyway, right? Well, yes and no. Misty might have been speaking the right safety language, but she failed to understand that her partner wasn't.

One of my favorite miscommunication mishap stories is a training example from my days at UPS. In the story, a new driver with no transportation experience had just completed orientation in Chicago. He was instructed to drive a tractor-trailer to the rail yard, drop the trailer off, and take the cab back. Any seasoned driver would have known that meant to leave the trailer full of freight and return with only the tractor. Imagine his supervisor's surprise when the rookie driver returned, confused, in a Yellow Cab with a hefty fare.

ONE OF THE MOST POWERFUL WAYS TO BREAK THE ACCIDENT CHAIN IS BY USING YOUR OWN VOICE.

The lesson here is to never assume that others know what you're talking about. Always consider your audience, and tailor your communication to them. Do they know the terms you're using? Do they have the proper frame of reference to understand your instructions? Most importantly, are you sure? All joking aside, when you're dealing with a safety situation, it's never a bad idea to ask someone to repeat instructions back to you, just to make sure you're on the same page.

YOU HAVE A SAFETY VOICE. USE IT.

One of the most powerful ways to break the accident chain is by using your own voice.

Remember the story about me standing behind my father and catching a saw with my forehead? I was young and didn't think to speak up at the time, but had I simply told my dad I was standing there, he would never have swung the saw the way he did in that moment, and we both would have been spared a lot of pain.

When it comes to safety, two words that every supervisor, employee, and parent needs to be able to say with courage and confidence are "stop" and "no." Remember the Challenger space shuttle disaster of 1986? It's common knowledge now that the O-rings on the shuttle were defective in cold weather, causing the devastating explosion. Unfortunately, it's extremely likely that many of the NASA staff knew about the O-rings' potential failure before the launch even happened. Had someone spoken up and said "Stop!" one of the most heartbreaking American tragedies could have been prevented. As the OSHA director in my earlier story and the example of the Canary Islands tragedy so powerfully illustrated, "stop" and "no" are two little words that have the power to save a lot of lives. Don't be afraid to use them.

COMMUNICATE CLEARLY

➡ Communication makes the difference between an accident that is allowed to happen and a zero-injury environment.

➡ We're rarely in total control of the circumstances that surround us, but we can be in control of the way we communicate.

➡ Safety communication extends far beyond the words we say; it also includes our actions.

➡ Communication is one area where carelessness and not thinking are closely linked.

SMART MOVE > Break the Accident Chain

USE YOUR OWN VOICE. TWO WORDS THAT EVERYONE NEEDS TO BE ABLE TO SAY WITH COURAGE AND CONFIDENCE ARE "STOP" AND "NO."

➡ Picture yourself as a member of a massive safety team. How can you play your part in the big picture of keeping yourself and everyone around you safe?

➡ Engineer out the risk of an accident with a simple, common safety language understood by everyone involved.

➡ Consider your audience, tailor your communication to them, and make sure your communication is a two-way street.

➡ Be open to observations and safety suggestions from others.

CHAPTER 6

TAKE A SLOWDOWN
(NOT A SHORTCUT)

My Granddaddy Pierce often shifted his old pickup truck's transmission from first gear straight to third. The engine would labor for a bit but gradually rumble over the forgotten second gear as we traveled into town, and I'll never forget the sound or the feel of that engine trying to catch up. When we asked why he skipped second gear, he would say, "I'm saving it till I need it." His quick wit and often rambunctious behavior were part of his charm. He had many accidents and injuries because of his impromptu shortcuts and sometimes-careless approach to life, but he sure was fun to be around. He was definitely an influence on my own interest in safety and the relationship between safety and risk.

Just as it was for my granddaddy in his old truck, one of the most tempting risks we take is the ever-available shortcut. Whether it's a questionable maneuver to climb the corporate ladder, cutting corners to earn a quota bonus faster, or simply looking for a quicker way to wrap up a job and get home, we've all searched for the easy way out at one time or another in our lives. We all want to be successful and accomplish certain goals, and from time to time, we've all wished there were a faster way to get to the finish line.

By definition, a shortcut is "a method or means of doing something more directly and quickly than, and often not so thoroughly as, by ordinary procedure." It's a wordy definition, but the key thing to notice here is the "not so thoroughly" part. Shortcuts look appealing. We think they'll save us time and money. We think they'll make our lives easier and less complicated. We think we won't have to work as hard if we can just eliminate a few steps here or there. But as with most things that fall into the category of "the grass isn't always greener on the other side," shortcuts are just that: appealing, enticing, alluring, and false. My dad often said, "If you don't have time to do it the right way the first time, what makes you think you'll have time to do it right the next time when you mess up and have to do it again?" Shortcuts almost always require more effort, time, and energy in the long run than if we'd simply done it the right way the first time.

SIMPLE VS. SHORT

But wait, aren't shortcuts sometimes more efficient? After all, our modern society can't get enough of the processes and gadgets that save time and boost productivity. What about the big push to simplify, simplify, simplify—didn't Steve Jobs build the Apple empire on making things more streamlined?

Well, yes. But there's a major difference between simplifying and taking a shortcut. Both work toward the end goal of saving time and energy, but they go about it two different ways. Simplifying pares a task or a process down to only its essentials; a shortcut eliminates those essentials in an attempt to save time and energy.

Picture two people on a reality television cooking show. They're both up to their elbows in flour, sugar, eggs, and specialty ingredients as they work to get a batch of chocolate chip cookies baked before the buzzer sounds. One contestant decides to simplify the recipe by adding only chocolate chips and omitting the walnuts he'd planned to use, which would have required time to chop and roast. The other contestant takes a frantic shortcut at the end and cuts the baking time in half, hoping for the best. When it's time for the judges to taste the cookies, one batch is perfectly moist and sweet, and nobody misses the walnuts; the other batch is still gooey and not fully cooked, practically inedible. The difference? One contestant eliminated an unnecessary step; the other eliminated an essential one.

Albert Einstein is quoted as saying, "Everything should be made as simple as possible, but not simpler." It's a fine line, isn't it?

Unfortunately, skipping the essentials to save time and effort can result in more than a bad batch of cookies. Just ask Walt, a production supervisor and self-described safety-conscious person I interviewed once in a bottling factory in Dallas, Texas.

One spring Saturday morning, Walt was wrapping up his favorite weekend routine: getting his yard into shape, just the way he liked it. He loved the sun on his back, the smell of the fresh cut grass, and the feeling of accomplishment after he finished with his work and stepped back to see the results of his labor.

On this particular day, Walt had just finished mowing his lawn and cranked up the weed eater to trim the edges around the fence line. He cut along the flowerbeds and up both sides of the driveway and then stopped to admire his work. He rested the weed eater against the back of his pickup, took off his safety glasses, and wiped the sweat from his face. He surveyed his work and noticed that he'd missed a spot near the

SHORTCUTS ALMOST ALWAYS REQUIRE MORE EFFORT, TIME, AND ENERGY IN THE LONG RUN THAN IF WE'D SIMPLY DONE IT THE RIGHT WAY THE FIRST TIME.

corner of the driveway. Walt's arms were tired, but he didn't want to leave the job unfinished. He reached for the weed eater, wiped it down to get a better grip, and walked over to finish the spot he'd missed. It would only take a swipe or two, he figured, so he didn't need to walk back to the truck and put his safety glasses back on.

Walt revved up the weed eater and swung it once, sending a rock directly into his eye. He described the sickening feeling of warm liquid oozing down his cheek so vividly that I actually felt the same sensation as he was telling the story.

At the emergency room, Walt didn't need his wife to tell him the news; he could tell by her face after she talked to the surgeon that he was going to lose the eye. Walt said they sat in silence in the hospital room for over an hour, trying to process what would happen next.

For years, Walt obsessed over how unfair it was that he lost his eye the one time he didn't protect it. After all, he was so safe most of the time. Even as he told me the story, he said that regret still crossed his mind every morning as he reached for the glass eye soaking in a cup of water next to his bed.

Walt was tired and ready to be done with his work, and he took a shortcut. Unfortunately, the ten steps he saved by not going back to the truck for his safety glasses cost him half his sight.

FROM SHORTCUT TO BAD HABIT

Our friend Walt didn't get a close call or a warning. His accident chain was just one link long, but not all shortcuts result in immediate tragedy, of course. Remember the One-Armed Farmer from Chapter 3? That shortcut he took by reaching his hand into the running baler to unclog it resulted in several close calls before it took his arm. He allowed his dangerous shortcut to become something even more dangerous: a bad habit. I'll always remember him saying, "I lost three gloves in that baler before it got me."

In all my years in the safety profession, I have heard countless stories of shortcuts becoming the preferred way to get the job done. This can be extremely dangerous on the jobsite because it often leads to others adopting the same behavior, increasing risk across the board. The first time a shortcut is taken, it's likely attempted by one person after carefully pondering the situation. When nothing bad happened right away as a result, the person repeats it over and over again, and others try it too. The shortcut method quickly becomes "how it's done," the perception of risk seems to just vaporize, and a dangerous complacency becomes the norm instead of the exception.

I once worked on a case that involved a heavy industrial press in a factory environment. Barry, the supervisor on the job, had a reputation for being accident prone; he'd lost a thumb on the job years before, and some people on the pressroom team were uncomfortable with his ability to lead the team.

The factory had just won a major contract with an international automobile manufacturer to produce metal parts for undercarriage frames. Overnight, the factory added a second shift and doubled its workforce. Overtime became a requirement, and Saturday work became routine. Quality, morale, and—you guessed it, safety—began to suffer.

A pressman named Michael was assigned to run a new, advanced press that had additional safety precautions built in; it required both hands to start the press, making it impossible for a worker to activate the equipment with his or her hand inside.

Barry saw these additional precautions as cumbersome and unnecessary. He removed the hood that protected the buttons from accidental activation and taped the one starter button into its activated position, essentially removing its built-in safety features and making it possible to operate the machine seated and with one hand. In Barry's mind, he was creating a more efficient process by eliminating steps.

Michael was uneasy at first with the modifications, but Barry showed him how much faster work would go without having to stop and operate the press with both hands. Michael quickly got the hang of it, and pretty soon, he stopped worrying about the risk and saw the benefits of working faster, reaching for materials with his right hand as he pressed the button with his left. With work going so quickly, he started dreaming about how he'd spend the production bonus he was sure to earn.

Just before quitting time, Michael noticed a piece of metal caught inside the press at an odd angle. He stood up and started to reach inside the press to grab it. Because Barry's modifications placed him so close to the unguarded activation button, his leg pushed against it, starting the press and crushing his hand and forearm in seconds.

Barry's shortcuts had eliminated everything that was put in place to protect Michael, putting him in danger for the sake of productivity. It only took one shift for Michael to become numb to the very real risks of Barry's shortcut and only one misstep for the shortcut to turn into tragedy.

Unfortunately, the consequences of Barry's unsafe modification and Michael's decision to take the shortcut didn't end there. Accidents almost always have a ripple effect of sorts, especially when they happen on the job.

Losing a hand, like Michael did, can also mean a dramatic change in how you provide for others and even care for yourself. Few families can go without the primary breadwinner for long, and strained finances test relationships in some of the toughest ways. Many times, the accident is only the beginning of the pain caused by a taking a shortcut.

IN A HURRY TO PLEASE

Shortcuts aren't always inspired by a need to expend less personal time and energy, cut corners, or cheat the system. Sometimes shortcuts are inspired by a real desire to improve a process, ease someone else's burden, or save a company time and money. And sometimes the pressure to perform—whether it's personally or professionally—can push us into an unintentional shortcut.

While working with an auto auction company years ago, I met with a district manager who came to me extremely frustrated that the company's string of 362 injury-free days was broken by what he described as sheer stupidity. He shook his head slowly as he told me that Robert, one of the detail employees, had somehow managed to stick a broken radio antenna up his nose. I must admit, it sounded pretty stupid to me at the time too.

The injury was bloody but fortunately somewhat minor, and Robert was back to work after a couple of days. I interviewed him to talk about what caused the accident and how it could have been prevented. It's part of my job to conduct interviews like this, but I was personally curious as to what stupidity had to have been brewing to make getting an antenna up the nose even possible.

Robert turned out to be a really interesting and intelligent guy. He explained that he'd been with the company several years, had worked his way up to his position, and took great pride in doing his part to increase the value of cars by making them shine. He showed me some of the very high-priced cars that were in rough condition and explained his role in getting them ready for the buyers.

Robert told me that this was his first incident in six years of cleaning cars. He even told me about some of the employees' shortcuts that he always avoids, like running a hand between the seats and risking getting cut by an unseen sharp object. He seemed just as baffled as anyone at how he could have stuck an antenna up his nose but also recognized that it could have been much worse if he had lost his eye instead.

He went on to explain that he was behind in his work and had been in a hurry—instead of walking around the hood of the car to buff the remaining wax, he bent way over and stretched to reach the other side of the hood and just happened to come down on the broken antenna.

Robert wasn't just an idiot taking a stupid shortcut. He was a caring individual who wanted to do the best-possible job to bring the highest dollar possible for his company. He talked about his two young boys that were his pride and joy and about how the days he missed from work due to the injury were the only days he had ever missed working in his life.

Was Robert's accident preventable? Of course. Was his shortcut out of laziness or lack of attention to detail? Not exactly. I'd say Robert's shortcut was more of an unintentional move that stemmed from lack of knowledge or awareness of his surroundings due to one important factor: being in a hurry.

Like Robert, when we get in a hurry, *even when it's for the "right" reasons,* we lose the ability to see and fully consider the risks associated with a shortcut. We become more focused on the finish line than the race itself. So how do we keep our need for speed aligned with our commitment to safety? M.O.S.T. is all about staying focused on the process, not the scoreboard or the finish line.

TAKE A SLOWDOWN

What if when we wanted to take a shortcut, we trained ourselves to slow down instead?

I'm not talking about slowing so much that it holds up traffic or halts production (which creates its own dangers). I'm talking about slowing down just enough to think about why a shortcut sounds like a good idea and understanding what your real goal is in the first place. If we slow down to truly clarify the basics of the task, we can make adjustments to simplify—leaving the essentials intact—rather than choosing a shortcut that invites risk for ourselves and those around us.

A SHORTCUT IS AN ACCELERATED WAY OF DOING SOMETHING, AND WHEN YOU SPEED THINGS UP, YOU GENERALLY LOSE SOME ASPECT OF CONTROL.

Slowing down even a little bit helps us regain or maintain control over our situation. We've established early on that speed leads to loss of control. Remember when I fell off the front porch as a kid in my rocking chair? A shortcut is an accelerated way of doing something, and when you speed things up, you generally lose some aspect of control.

We naturally respond to risk by slowing down. Think of crossing a stream by hopping from rock to rock, or walking across an icy parking lot. Our bodies and minds automatically sense the danger in the situation and cause us to walk slowly and intentionally. When we're tempted to speed up, that means we're forgetting the risks involved. Sound familiar?

When you're tempted to take a shortcut, that's your cue that you're not considering risk, and it's time to slow down and figure out how to simplify instead. Slowing down sharpens our awareness of our surroundings and brings the "right way" into focus.

SLOWING DOWN AND METHOD ORIENTED

In my career, I've consulted with several recycling clients. Recycling yards can be potentially dangerous environments, where workers must be particularly vigilant about safety. At this particular recycling yard, an employee named Terry was tasked with removing a gas tank from an old wrecked car before sending it through the shredder. Technically, the tanks are required to be removed prior to being brought to the recycling yard, but from time to time, a few make it through, and the tanks must be removed.

Terry was siphoning gas from the tank little by little before removing it, an assignment that proved to be a tedious task. He thought it would be easier and faster if he drilled a hole in the gas tank to drain the gasoline. The car was already up on a hydraulic lift, after all. He chose an electric drill with a steel bit and went to work; the sparks from the friction ignited the gasoline and the tank exploded, leaving Terry with burns over 80 percent of his body. If he had slowed down to think about his shortcut, he would have realized the likelihood of sparks from the drill igniting the gasoline inside.

SLOWING DOWN SHARPENS OUR AWARENESS OF OUR SURROUNDINGS AND BRINGS THE "RIGHT WAY" INTO FOCUS.

Slowing down instead of finding a shortcut is a key element of the M.O.S.T. system. Slowing down gives us the time and space to follow safety procedures, eliminate risk, and keep essential steps in the process. Staying Method Oriented and using Safety Thinking saves us from accidents like Terry's, keeping us in line with the processes that are in place to protect us from risks we might not see or understand right away.

Staying Method Oriented can also mean following our own set of processes to stay organized, prepared, and safe. Always keeping your car keys in the same place in the house ensures they're easily and quickly accessible in an emergency, for example. Paying bills on the same day every month ensures that you'll never overlook a due date.

Vince Lombardi once said, "Winning isn't a sometime thing; it's an all the time thing. You don't win once in a while; you don't do things right once in a while; you do them right all the time. Winning is a habit. Unfortunately, so is losing." Substitute the word "safety" for "winning" in the quote above, and you'll see that it's just as applicable.

STUPIDITY STOPPER

TAKE A SLOWDOWN (NOT A SHORTCUT)

➡ Shortcuts almost always require more effort, time, and energy in the long run than just doing a task the right way.

➡ A shortcut is not the same as simplifying.
- Simplifying pares down to only the essentials.
- Shortcuts eliminate essentials in an attempt to save time and energy.

➡ Shortcuts are the gateway to bad safety habits.

➡ When we get in a hurry, we can't see the risks associated with a shortcut. We become more focused on the finish line than the race itself.

SMART MOVE ❯ **Break the Accident Chain**

WHEN WE'RE TEMPTED TO SPEED UP, THAT MEANS WE'RE FORGETTING THE RISKS INVOLVED. SLOWING DOWN SHARPENS OUR AWARENESS OF OUR SURROUNDINGS AND BRINGS THE "RIGHT WAY" INTO FOCUS.

➡ When you're tempted to take a shortcut, it's time to slow down and focus on doing the right thing instead.

➡ Slow down and give yourself the time and space to follow safety procedures, eliminate risk, and keep essential steps in the process.

CHAPTER 7

TRAIN YOUR
SAFETY AUTOPILOT

I heard this story at a gun-carry permit class years ago. It has stuck with me ever since, probably because the story hit especially close to home for me since I had young grandkids at the time.

In the story, a man—let's call him Nate—was like many of us in the class and kept a gun for home protection. He had taken it to the shooting range a couple of times but didn't use it regularly. One lazy Saturday afternoon, he got his pistol out to clean it. Years had passed since he'd been to a gun safety class or shooting range, but he was reasonably confident that he remembered the steps involved. Nate found a football game on TV and sat down at the kitchen table to clean the gun. One by one, his kids wandered into the adjacent living room and sat down to watch the game. He didn't stop what he was doing because he wanted his kids to be comfortable around firearms. Plus, he'd been extra careful to open the receiver and check for any ammo in the chamber. Unfortunately, he skipped a commonsense gun-cleaning rule: to first completely remove (not just check) the magazine clip that holds the bullets. When he first checked the chamber, he found it empty; but when he released the spring action to close it again, he unknowingly fed a bullet into the chamber he'd just checked.

Now, instead of cleaning a harmless weapon, he was unknowingly handling a loaded gun just a few feet from where his three bright, healthy kids sat watching TV, something he would never, ever have done intentionally. Everyone in that room was in extremely real and present danger as he sat at the table with a loaded gun pointed directly at his children. He was ignoring the most important and most commonsense rule of firearm safety: never, ever point a gun—loaded or not—toward anything you do not intend to shoot.

You can probably guess what happened next. While Nate held the weapon in one hand and wiped it down with an oily rag, the gun fired, killing his middle son as he sat next to his sister on the couch.

No matter where he is now, I'm certain that Nate still hasn't forgiven himself for his mistake and probably revisits that day again and again in his mind and heart. I know I would.

This tragedy brings up a question you might have been asking yourself throughout this book. Knowing how easy it is to mix up the steps in a process or fail to do something correctly on the first try, how can we possibly be expected to remember every single safety rule and procedure all the time?

Being method oriented and applying safety thinking helps us remember to first remove the magazine clip holding the bullets and always point the gun in a safe direction.

When we unpack the accident chain from that tragic day, we see several of the links we've talked about before: Nate was rusty on his gun safety rules and might not have had the proper training to handle the weapon he was cleaning in the first place. He might have been distracted by the game on TV. He might have simply fallen into a bad habit learned long ago or lost focus on the task at hand. We'll never know exactly what happened, but no matter what links were building in the accident chain, one simple, absolutely controllable factor could have changed everything. If Nate had just obeyed the one ultimate gun safety rule of never pointing a gun toward anything you do not intend to shoot—*even after he was "sure" it wasn't loaded*—the entire tragedy would have been prevented. Sure, Nate might still have accidentally discharged the bullet and put a hole in the floor. His kids would have been understandably shaken, and he would probably have been scared to death by his close call. But he would still have his son, and he'd have a dramatic cautionary tale to tell instead of a lifetime of regret and pain.

YOUR SAFETY AUTOPILOT

Let's face it: we all go on autopilot, like Nate probably did, from time to time when we're completing a task that has become familiar or seems mundane. We all forget how to do things, learn improper methods, or fall into bad habits. From factory workers to nurses and restaurant chefs to administrative professionals, we all act sometimes without giving our full attention to safety and process. I'm not here to tell you that's wrong. I'm here to tell you that's natural. And because it's bound to happen, that means we have to plan for it.

Most of us can remember driving a familiar route to work or school, getting to our destination and realizing that we don't recall what we did during the drive. Once we've driven a route numerous times, our minds go into autopilot mode, and our bodies perform the required actions without conscious thought. It isn't that we were being unsafe during the drive; it's just that we've developed the routine or habit of making that particular drive and, as far as following the correct route and speed limits, we no longer need to give it active thought.

Similarly, each of us can construct a personal Safety Autopilot if we just choose to train it and engage it. In modern airplanes, the autopilot can, in most cases, fly the plane straighter and more level than the most seasoned pilot. It does not suffer from human factors like fatigue, distractions, anger, depression, or fear. It has no predisposition for stupidity. The autopilot just flies the plane with precision and consistency. How do we train our own Safety Autopilot to automatically engage the safe habits that override the stupidity links in an accident chain?

A Safety Autopilot is developed much like a muscle. In order to build our muscles, we exercise them regularly. The more we use our muscles, the stronger they become. Like a muscle, we develop a strong Safety Autopilot by using it. First we must determine the safety behaviors that are important, and then we use those behaviors every single time they're needed.

For example, we develop the Safety Autopilot of eliminating cell phone distractions while driving by turning off our cell phone every single time we get into the driver's seat of a car. Soon it becomes routine, and we no longer even consider picking up our phones while driving. We know that even an emergency phone call can wait the few seconds or minutes it would take to drive the car to the side of the road or to a parking lot where we can stop and safely handle the call.

I'm a firm believer that what you believe is what you will become. Consciously cultivating safe habits and practicing M.O.S.T. in daily life inoculates against stupidity, ensuring the Safety Autopilot checks in to help break the accident chain when we are distracted, tired, or otherwise checked out.

HABIT

One of my favorite nuggets of wisdom on the subject of habit—good and bad—is this widely shared poem that has been quoted in motivational business literature for decades. It simply and brilliantly illustrates the importance of training your Safety Autopilot.

WHO AM I?

I am your constant companion.
I am your greatest helper or heaviest burden.
I will push you onward or drag you down to failure.
I am completely at your command.
Half the things you do you might just as well turn
    over to me,
And I will do them quickly and correctly.
I am easily managed; you must merely be firm with me.
Show me exactly how you want something done,
And after a few lessons I will do it automatically.
I am the servant of all great people, and alas,
Of all failures as well.
Those who are great, I have made great.
Those who are failures, I have made failures.
I am not a machine, though I work with all the precision
    of a machine plus the intelligence of a human being.
You may run me for profit or run me for ruin,
It makes no difference to me.
Take me, train me, be firm with me,
And I will put the world at your feet.
Be easy with me and I will destroy you.
Who am I?
I am HABIT!
—Author Unknown

With a strong Safety Autopilot, safe behaviors become second nature, like brushing your teeth. You don't need to remind yourself to uncap the tube of toothpaste and squeeze it onto the brush. You don't need a checklist to remember to move the brush around in your mouth or to rinse the brush when you're finished. It's second nature to you because you've practiced doing it the right way so many times that the sequence comes to you automatically. The same goes for tasks like driving to work or running a load of laundry. You don't have to put your address into your GPS every time you commute to and from your job or repeatedly look up what temperature settings to use for a load of towels. You just do it without thinking.

JUST AS YOU CAN DO UNSAFE THINGS WITHOUT THINKING, YOUR SAFETY AUTOPILOT MAKES IT POSSIBLE TO DO THE SAFE THING WITHOUT THINKING TOO.

Your Safety Autopilot is probably already working for you every time you look both ways before crossing the street, hold a chopping knife away from your hand, or reach for an oven mitt automatically before grabbing a hot pan from the oven. When it's truly engaged, the Safety Autopilot is stronger than our desire to take a shortcut, get sucked in by a distraction, or shift our focus from the task at hand. Just as you can do unsafe things without thinking, your Safety Autopilot makes it possible to do the safe thing without thinking too.

YOUR INTERNAL COMPASS

As a navigational tool, we know that a compass always points north, but how does it know which way to go? The red magnetized end of the compass needle is influenced by the magnetic field of the North Pole, causing it to turn north. I've always found it fascinating and profound that the unseen forces in the natural world—magnetism, electricity, and gravity—are the most consistent and unwavering, and more powerful than anything man can create. They establish order on the Earth, from the push and pull of the tides to keeping the planets in orbit.

I used to spend hours as a kid playing with my dad's compass, fascinated by its unwavering ability to find due north. On the other hand, the weather vane on my grandfather's barn would twist and turn in response to whichever way the wind was blowing.

I believe that the unseen forces in our own lives can be just as powerful as the magnetic forces causing the compass to point north. Whenever your Safety Autopilot influences your behavior, your Internal Compass is the unseen guiding force that sets its course. Your Internal Compass is like a sixth sense that tells right from wrong; your Safety Autopilot follows that direction on your behalf.

My Grandmother Pierce taught me to love watching the stars. We'd spend hours at night sitting on a blanket in a back hay field on my grandparents' small Georgia farm figuring out constellations. I learned that each night and day, constellations like the Big Dipper and Cassiopeia slowly turn counter-clockwise around the North Star in perfect harmony on courses they have traveled for millions of years. With my grandmother's help, I learned how to orient myself by first locating the Big Dipper and then tracing the path to the bright North Star.

YOUR INTERNAL COMPASS IS LIKE A SIXTH SENSE THAT TELLS RIGHT FROM WRONG; YOUR SAFETY AUTOPILOT FOLLOWS THAT DIRECTION ON YOUR BEHALF.

With the North Star as your anchor, mapping the outline of constellations is as simple as connecting the dots between the right stars until a shape suddenly appears in the night sky. I believe the same is true when it comes to following proper safety protocol. For example, the right and safe way to lift is to plan the lift, then get close to the object, and use the muscles of the legs and arms to lift and protect the back. When the correct methods are linked together, safety happens. Once we learn how to align with the North Star—our Internal

Compass—the constellations of our actions all fall into place safely.

As with any navigational instrument, using your Internal Compass to keep your Safety Autopilot on course requires constant adjustments and recalibrations. This is where close calls, conscious awareness, past experience, and training come in. You might have heard the famous quote by the Greek philosopher Heraclitus, who wrote in 550 BC, "No man ever steps in the same river twice, for it is not the same river, and he is not the same man." We are constantly changing, evolving, and becoming, and those experiences along the way help cultivate our Internal Compass.

As the supervisor in a small, rural nursing home, my mother had a famous saying: "You get what you expect and what you inspect." The same applies to your Safety Autopilot. The expectations you set for yourself must become a part of who you are, and you alone must hold yourself accountable. Just as a long-haul truck driver must make constant micro-adjustments at the steering wheel to stay on the road, we must also self-inspect our thinking moment by moment in order to constantly align and realign our behaviors with our self-set expectations.

To keep your Internal Compass and Safety Autopilot engaged and in working order, you must be willing to remove carelessness and not thinking like you would remove weeds from a garden. It's a constant task but one that is much simpler with regular attention.

A quick and easy way to check in with your Internal Compass is to try all six senses: Does it sound right? Does it feel right? Does it smell, look, and taste right? And most importantly, does my gut confirm that it is—or isn't—right?

DOING RIGHT, ALL THE TIME

I think it goes without saying that the Internal Compass extends beyond Safety Thinking too. Your Internal Compass is your gut feeling that tells you right from wrong. As parents, leaders, supervisors, and mentors, we're all responsible for not only cultivating that sense within ourselves, but in the people we care for as well. A strong sense of right and wrong serves as a lifelong guide in personal safety, decision-making, and moral dilemmas—the moments that define our character.

In my parents' house growing up, there were two clearly worn paths from our house: one led from the front door to the mailbox; the other led out the back door to the outhouse. Getting where you needed to go was simple: you simply picked the right path and stayed on it.

I use this example often when talking about the Internal Compass. Getting where you want to go—whether that's a zero-injury work environment, financial stability, or a committed relationship—means intentionally choosing the correct path or course of action and staying on it until you get there.

Even as we practice following our own Internal Compass, we have a responsibility in our roles as parents, supervisors, coaches, and even friends to help influence others' compass needles. When I work with supervisors, I describe it as "super vision," a special ability to address not only the day-to-day details of keeping employees safe, but also the big-picture view of safety culture, productivity, and excellence in quality and service. Just as the magnetic pull of the North Pole can pull a compass needle north, so can we influence others toward doing the right thing all the time, whether it's by our leadership, our example, or both. As a father, I certainly made this a priority when my children were young. I knew that if I could help shape their personal Internal Compasses, they would ultimately be pulled to do the right thing as they gained independence and found themselves in positions to make their own decisions.

My dad instilled this "always point north" mentality in us from an early age. Though deer are plentiful in the South now, in the 1960s, they had been overhunted and were nearly extinct. During that time, a stocking initiative to increase the deer population in Georgia was underway, which proved to be successful; hunting was once again encouraged to begin keeping the population in check. When I was in high school during this period, my friends and I would talk about deer sightings like rare occasions. People hunted for years before finally getting one, and many hunters broke the law by killing deer out of season. Not my dad though.

I distinctly remember meeting up with Dad and my brother back at our truck one cold December morning when we'd been hunting since before sunrise. The game warden drove past us as we put our guns away, and we talked for a bit. We commiserated with him for a minute over our bad luck with deer sightings, and he went on his way. After the warden drove off, Dad told us he'd actually seen a buck down the logging road where we'd come into the woods. My brother and I were completely flabbergasted as to why he didn't shoot it.

Dad simply explained that while it was deer season in our county, it wasn't deer season in the next county over. Being so close to the county line, he couldn't be sure which county it was in, so he didn't shoot. His answer made perfect sense to him but no sense whatsoever to two kids eager to bag our first buck.

We pointed out that Dad could have shot the deer anyway and just told the game warden that he'd done it in our county. I remember my dad nodding slowly, saying, "You're right. I could have. But I'd rather be sure I'm doing the right thing than take the chance of breaking the law." This example of a strong Internal Compass has stayed with me my entire life.

I closed the previous chapter with one of my favorite Vince Lombardi quotes about doing the right thing, all the time. That quote resonates with me personally because of my own upbringing: my own dad used to always say, "If a job's worth doing, it's worth doing right." This theme has influenced my approach to safety as well as to the development of the M.O.S.T. system and has truly touched every aspect of my life.

Over the years, I have found the compass illustration to be very helpful when explaining the Method Oriented piece of M.O.S.T. Handheld compasses are instruments used in orienteering exercises, timed competitive events that require participants to navigate through rough terrain to find specific checkpoints using only a map and compass. The compass is essential to the sport, as it establishes a fixed reference point for the orienteers by always pointing toward the North Pole. No matter where the orienteer is standing, they always know where they stand in relation to north.

When a person is Method Oriented, they are committed to doing the job the right way, every time. They are oriented toward a specific method. On the job, that might mean hospital housekeeping staff placing a caution sign on a wet floor after mopping it, following the same method every single time until it becomes a second-nature habit, alerting others to the risk of slips and falls.

When it comes to safety, it's more important to listen to your Internal Compass and train your Safety Autopilot to do things the right, safe way every time than to take a chance and risk injury, property damage, or death. When we talk about M.O.S.T., the second part of the equation is Safety Thinking. Our Internal Compass and Safety Autopilot are responsible for making that Safety Thinking our default setting, leading us to "do the right thing," no matter what.

So many times, we fall into unsafe habits even when we know the right way to do a task. We simply start doing something the wrong way a few times, and before long, that becomes our default habit. Once, during a company training at a shipping warehouse, I set a large, empty box on the stage and asked a man from the audience to come up and demonstrate how to properly lift it. He joined me on the stage, but before he lifted the box, he paused and asked with a sheepish grin, "Do you want me to do it the right way or the way I always do it?" Despite knowing the right methods, he had trained his autopilot to lift boxes in a way that put his back at risk for a strain every single day on the job.

We've discussed in other chapters how the way we think dictates the way we act. If we train ourselves to think about safety, then safe actions will follow. When I talk about the Internal Compass and Safety Autopilot in my trainings, I often refer to the expression, "Give a man a fish, and he will eat today; teach him to fish, and he will never be hungry." When we practice cultivating our Safety Thinking to a point where it becomes second nature, we're equipped to stay safe in any situation, no matter what the circumstances.

Like my father, my mother had a powerful influence on me when it came to doing the right thing all the time. She was strict but always supportive and unconditionally loving, no matter what kind of trouble I'd stumbled into or how stupid my mistakes might have been. She was famous for saying, "Your sins will find you out," meaning that even "just this one time" exceptions have a way of coming back to bite you, whether it's an immediate mishap or the slow erosion of good habits that ultimately lead to consequences. Never fail to buckle your seatbelt. Never drink alcohol if the disease of addiction hides in the shadows. Never smoke, use drugs, or take just-this-once risk you know to be unsafe.

As a pilot, I have taken off hundreds and hundreds of times but only after going carefully through a printed checklist. Even though the steps never change, I will never take off without religiously completing it. Why? The risk is just too great. One single oversight can mean the difference between a safe flight and a "never again" experience.

I hear a lot of stories from truck drivers and transportation industry professionals, and it's still shocking to me how many of the tractor trailer accidents I investigate involve the failure to wear seatbelts. For most of us, the seatbelt habit has become absolutely automatic, thanks in large part to successful national safety campaigns launched in the 1980s. Truck drivers can be an unfortunate example of letting the Safety Autopilot become lax and inviting tragic stupidity. It's easy to feel invincible surrounded by so much power and metal; they often rationalize not wearing a seatbelt using the logic that in a highway accident, the massive truck cab is probably the safest place to be. They couldn't be more wrong. Without a seatbelt, the impact of even a minor crash can easily throw a truck driver around the cab (or out of it entirely) with deadly force, even if the body of the truck sustains minimal damage. Unfortunately, that fact is proven every single day by those who choose not to make seatbelt wearing a part of their Safety Autopilot.

A strong Internal Compass and Safety Autopilot are more powerful and lasting than any written warning or safety message will ever be. No matter what external circumstances apply, training yourself to practice safety instinctively can help keep your unfortunate stupid mistakes from becoming tragic, life-changing events. Just ask Nate, the man who accidentally shot his own son.

STUPIDITY STOPPER

TRAIN YOUR SAFETY AUTOPILOT

➡ Inside all of us is a Safety Autopilot if we just choose to develop and engage it.

➡ Your Safety Autopilot lays the groundwork for safe behavior to happen and keeps stupidity at bay.

➡ The Internal Compass is the guiding force that sets the Safety Autopilot's course.

➡ A strong Internal Compass and Safety Autopilot are more powerful and lasting than any written warning or safety message will ever be.

SMART MOVE **Break the Accident Chain**

NO MATTER WHAT EXTERNAL CIRCUMSTANCES APPLY, TRAINING YOURSELF TO INSTINCTIVELY PRACTICE SAFETY CAN HELP KEEP YOUR STUPID MISTAKES FROM BECOMING TRAGIC, LIFE-CHANGING EVENTS.

➡ Using your Internal Compass to keep your Safety Autopilot active requires constant adjustment and recalibration, an ongoing effort to remove carelessness and not thinking from the equation.

➡ When we simply train ourselves to follow our survival instincts and keep accident prevention on our radar without exception, safety naturally follows.

CHAPTER 8

JUST DON'T DO IT

Sometimes the most effective accident prevention isn't wearing PPE, or being process oriented, or following a checklist. Many times, the best way to keep an accident from happening is to do nothing.

What do I mean by that exactly? I mean that when we evaluate the task at hand and realize it's beyond our grasp or our experience or our tools, we just shouldn't do it. Simple as that. There is a special wisdom in knowing what you don't know, whether that means calling in an expert for advice before you attempt a complex home repair, seeking additional training before jumping into a work project, or just not attempting a task that requires skills, stamina, or strength you might not have in the first place.

The average person would never attempt to perform a surgery or fly a plane without the proper equipment and training. Why, then, do so many smart people get hurt or even lose their lives attempting other "out of their league" tasks every year? Why is YouTube so full of videos that make us say, "Oh my gosh, I can't believe he's doing that!" and then cover our eyes or laugh hysterically (or both)?

You see, when stupidity kicks in, we think pretty highly of ourselves. We see someone perform a new task on the job and think, "Well, I could do that." We see something that needs to be done around the house and we'd rather "get in there and figure it out" than spend money to hire a professional or simply admit we don't know what we're doing. Or the most dangerous of all, we take a puzzled look at the task at hand, turn to the person standing next to us, toss the instructions in the garbage, and say, "How hard could it be?"

Knowing that you don't have the skills or equipment to do a task and then doing it anyway is not thinking and carelessness in equal parts. From operating power tools without prior instruction to trying to lift a heavy piece of furniture with no help, sometimes it seems like people are

THERE IS A SPECIAL WISDOM IN KNOWING WHAT YOU DON'T KNOW.

just asking for accidents to happen—and in a way, they are. One of my favorite accident investigation quotes came from a man I interviewed after he'd lost his finger on the job. When I asked him what he'd learned from the accident, he simply said, "I learned I shoulda done what I already knew." When we jump into a task knowing we're not ready to take it on, we're building a strong and fast accident chain. My Granddaddy Pierce used to call it "playing the wild."

In the 1980s, I worked on a case that took place in a food manufacturing plant. Two workers were in charge of cleaning the facility on weekends and were expected to clean the machines inside and out for the upcoming week. They were paid a flat rate for the job, no matter how long it took; naturally, they started looking for ways to make the work go faster.

The chemical compound they used to clean the insides of the machines was a liquid they poured in and then flushed out. The outsides were scrubbed by hand, which took much longer. On this particular day, they decided to save time and use the interior solution to do the entire job—it seemed like a stronger chemical, and they hoped it would cut down on the elbow grease required to get the machines spotless. They wore gloves and were extra careful with the chemical. Sure enough, they were finished in half the time.

As they stood back admiring their work, one of the men felt something strange on his leg. They both looked down at the places where the chemicals had splashed on their pants and shoes. They saw big holes where the cleaner had burned through the fabric and even the leather of their boots. They soon realized the solution had also caused third-degree burns on their legs, faces, and hands.

As they rushed to the hospital, they grabbed the SDS (Safety Data Sheets) for the chemical they'd used. The sheets detailed all of the precautions for using the solution, including hazmat-grade full-body protection, as the chemical destroys skin and tissue without any sensation of pain. They not only lacked the proper equipment to be handling the chemical; they lacked the knowledge and understanding of how to keep themselves safe.

OVER YOUR HEAD

A friend of my wife's had hired professionals to hang Christmas lights and decorations on her family's three-story house, upping the ante on their holiday display to the delight of the neighborhood. A week after Christmas had come and gone, Barbara and her husband, Dan, made last-minute plans to visit their daughter in Florida. Not wanting to have workers at their house while they were away, Dan decided to take the lights down himself the day before they were scheduled to leave. He was never much of a handyman at home, but this task just didn't seem so tough. After all, he'd watched the crew put the lights up back in November, and it didn't seem that they had any special skills beyond his own. The only thing they had that he didn't was a fancy extension ladder. His work might be slower going, but it would also be free and fast.

Barbara remembers questioning Dan as he laced up his shoes at the top of the stairs that morning. He'd decided that rather than borrow an extension ladder, he'd just climb out an upstairs window to access the tin roof over the porch. He told Barbara he'd prepared for the job by wearing rubber-soled tennis shoes so he wouldn't slip. She'd actually thought he was joking at first, but he pointed out that the pitch of the porch roof didn't seem very steep—almost flat, in fact—and that the job was so simple, it would be a waste of money to hire the crew again.

Dan stepped through the upstairs window and tested his footing on the roof. He called to Barbara and told her it was a little slick but not dangerous and that he'd be done in no time.

Dan found the pitch to be much steeper than it looked from the ground and took extra care to lie on his side to keep his center of gravity low. As the job went on, the process was going smoothly, and he was becoming more confident; he tried sitting up and scooting along the edge of the roof, which made the job go even faster. Barbara watched from the front yard, relieved that taking down the lights was proving to be as simple as Dan predicted. After wrapping several strings of lights, Dan seemed more confident in his abilities. He stood up slowly, just as he'd seen the professional crew do, and turned around to put the lights in the storage box. In doing so, he lost his footing and fell from a standing position, landing on his hip on the brick steps twelve feet below.

The injury required several surgeries, and his hospital stay was extended due to an infection he contracted as he was healing. All in all, he was in the hospital for nearly a month. Dan never regained full mobility in his hip and will walk with a cane for the rest of his life. When my wife stopped by to deliver a meal during his recovery, he told her, "I just wish I could relive that one day. I had no business being out on that roof. If I'd just left it to the professionals, I'd still be doing all the things I thought I'd be doing for a long time yet, like hiking with my grandkids."

Now, Dan was no dummy. He absolutely knew better than to just step out onto the tin roof of the porch and remain standing. He recognized that move as being way too risky and started out cautiously on his side. As his confidence grew, however, he started taking bigger and bigger risks with his body even though he was in over his head, not recognizing that he was putting his life in danger.

Studies show that an unskilled person is actually more likely to become overconfident in his or her own abilities than even a skilled professional. It's harder than it seems to know what you don't know. It isn't always obvious that we're not up to the task or that external factors present too much risk to proceed safely.

I, too, am guilty of being overconfident, getting in over my head, and pushing through anyway.

In the aviation world, pilots call this phenomenon "get-home-itis," where the desire to get home on schedule overrides your ability to assess risk and temporarily erases what you know about keeping yourself safe.

There comes a point in instrument-rated pilots' training where they learn to fly a plane using only the instruments on the dash, enabling them to fly in the clouds with zero visibility. When I reached that point, I became much more comfortable with pushing through cloud buildups rather than navigating around them; I also became much more comfortable with the risk involved. Bumpy rides stopped being scary and became more normal to me. I was more bold and confident, but I didn't think I was capable of stupidity. I was wrong.

This confidence growth spurt—and that's what it really was—happened around the time I had gained 750 hours as a pilot. I've since learned that a surprisingly high number of fatal aviation accidents happen to pilots at that critical experience level, and I now understand why: we get in over our heads, and we don't recognize it.

On this particular day in the summer of 2001, I was preparing to fly out of Florida's Ocala airport. The weather radar showed the beginning signs of a scattered thunderstorm buildup in my path, with a stronger line of storms predicted to form. It looked like my window of opportunity for getting back to Nashville on time was closing fast.

Confident in my flying skills, I decided that if I left immediately, I'd be able to fly through the clouds before they became dangerous. After all, my vintage plane (a meticulously maintained 1966 Mooney) was in top-notch mechanical condition. I knew the storm scope in its dash wasn't as sophisticated as the equipment on board modern planes, so I made contact with a very helpful controller and trusted that he would help steer me through the clouds before the dangerous storms formed. There were two other small planes in my vicinity and on my frequency, headed along the same route. One was a little ahead of me and reported that he had made it through the line of building thunderstorms with no trouble; the other had already made the decision to turn back—a wise move. The controller helped me find new headings as my ride became bumpier, but he also told me that the "big irons" (commercial jets) were starting to fly around or above the storm and suggested I do the same.

Just then, all hell broke loose as the small Mooney suddenly shot up from 8,000 feet to an altitude of 10,000 feet in a matter of seconds. The pointer needle on the altimeter spun so fast I feared for the worst. My life literally flashed before my eyes, and I thought I was going down. My family was the only thing I could think of—all of the things I wanted to tell them. The wind kept the plane soaring upward out of control, changing direction as it went. I've never been so scared before or since. However, a quiet voice reminded me to stay calm and fly the airplane as turbulence continued to toss it around.

WE ALL GET IN OVER OUR HEADS FROM TIME TO TIME.

The whole event probably lasted two minutes or so, but it felt like hours. When I could stabilize the plane, I asked the controller to get me out of there. I chose the closest option he gave me: Cedar City Airport, about five miles away. It was nothing more than a remote fishing village with a few scattered houses, but it's one of the most treasured places I've ever visited. I've never been so happy to be on the ground as I was that evening.

My overconfidence and haste to get home blinded me to the fact that I had no business attempting such a risky flight in the first place. In doing so, I started an accident chain that nearly claimed my life.

TURN A STUPIDITY OPPORTUNITY INTO A LEARNING OPPORTUNITY

I am by no means suggesting that we should be afraid to try new things or that we shouldn't push ourselves to learn or perform outside of our comfort zones. "Just don't do it" doesn't have to mean walking away or giving up.

We all get in over our heads from time to time. Part of living the M.O.S.T. system is simply learning to see that moment clearly: recognizing when our skill, experience, or physical limitations don't match up with the task at hand and then acting on that insight.

Knowing what you don't know can mean asking for further instruction, requesting assistance, or simply slowing down to better assess the situation, much like we discussed in Chapter 6. Asking a seasoned coworker to demonstrate a task before you try it yourself can not only keep you from hurting yourself, but also build your own skill set in the process. And don't forget, YouTube can show you more than silly stupidity; spending five minutes watching a valuable home repair tutorial online can save you time and money and can often prevent serious injury or property damage.

When we consciously recognize the limits of our knowledge and expertise, we open ourselves to learning new things—even if that new thing is the phone number of a reliable handyman that keeps us off the roof and out of the electrical wiring at home. When we know for certain we have the essential skills and equipment in place for the task, we're more likely to achieve success.

STUPIDITY STOPPER

JUST DON'T DO IT

➡ When stupidity kicks in, we tend to overestimate our abilities.

➡ When we jump into a task we're not equipped to perform, we're building a strong and fast accident chain.

➡ It isn't always obvious that we're not up to the task or that external factors present too much risk to proceed safely.

SMART MOVE **Break the Accident Chain**

WE ALL GET IN OVER OUR HEADS FROM TIME TO TIME. PART OF LIVING THE M.O.S.T. SYSTEM IS RECOGNIZING WHEN OUR SKILL, EXPERIENCE, OR PHYSICAL LIMITATIONS DON'T MATCH UP WITH THE TASK AT HAND AND THEN ACTING ON THAT INSIGHT.

➡ Be absolutely certain you have the essential skills and equipment in place for the task, even if that means not attempting to do it yourself.

➡ "Just don't do it" doesn't have to mean walking away or giving up.

➡ When a task is beyond your skill or presents too much risk, ask for further instruction, request assistance, or simply slow down to better assess the situation.

CONCLUSION

STOP. THINK.

I hope you've found this book to be helpful in fine-tuning your sense of safety and in giving you a more in-depth understanding of the principles behind my M.O.S.T. system. However, none of the ideas and concepts in this book will do you a bit of good if you don't follow this final and most important guideline. It's the simplest of all but also the hardest to remember. Are you ready?

Just stop and think.

Whether it's before a major decision, when encountering a new situation or task, in a moment of stress, or when something just doesn't feel right, a simple pause can sharpen your safety sense and make the difference between smooth sailing and a life-changing injury, accident, or tragedy.

Pausing to evaluate and question your situation forces your brain to reset, even briefly; it can bring a bad habit into focus, calm panicked or rushed thinking, kick-start your Safety Autopilot, and most importantly, reveal your own human stupidity in action. It's always worth it.

Maybe you're speeding along in your car with your eyes glued to your cell phone instead of the road; maybe you're coming to the close of your shift, and you've gone into zombie mode, your attention wandering anywhere but on the job. Stopping to think can eliminate distractions and bring focus to your surroundings, like I discussed in Chapter 4. Or say you're flustered and frustrated, and everything seems to be going wrong on the job as your blood pressure rises and your coworkers look on. Stopping to think could help you fully recognize the danger in a close call or help you slow your actions and avoid a dangerous shortcut.

You can train yourself to handle any situation safely by simply stopping, thinking, and asking yourself:

How long would it take to do the proven safe thing?

In Walt's case from Chapter 6, it would have taken ten seconds to walk back to his truck and put on safety glasses; instead, he lost his eye to a flying rock kicked up by his own weed eater.

What are the consequences of continuing risky behavior?

For Brian the One-Armed Farmer in Chapter 3, stopping to think about losing three gloves in the baler might have saved his arm if he'd seen those close calls for what they were: very specific warnings.

Why am I doing what I know not to do?

My friend Dave would have been wise to stop and ask himself this question before investing in the too-good-to-be-true oil venture from Chapter 1; Dan would still be able to walk unassisted if he'd just called a professional to handle a job he wasn't qualified to tackle, as seen in Chapter 8. If you answer this question with, "It'll go faster," or "I'm stressed," or even "I don't know," those are red flags to change your course and break the accident chain.

How important is it to keep doing what I'm doing?

Remember Amy, the teen driver from the book's introduction? Weighing the importance of a simple text message against the possibility of killing someone with her car surely would have inspired her to leave her phone in her purse or pocket until she reached her destination.

Am I breaking a known safety rule?

If Ed from Chapter 1 had stopped to think and consider not just the "what" of the lock-out safety protocol but also the "why," he would never have climbed inside the pulpwood shredder without locking out the power source—a mistake that cost him his life.

What does common sense tell me to do? What is my gut feeling about this?

Nate from Chapter 7 would have avoided the greatest of all tragedies—the loss of a child—had he simply stopped for a moment and allowed his Safety Autopilot and Internal Compass to guide the gun away from his own children and point it in a safe direction.

How do the people around me affect what I'm doing and vice versa?

If Misty at the nursing home in Chapter 5 had stopped to consider that her coworker and patient needed to play an active role in her lift, she could have taken the two seconds to clarify her safety language and save her own back in the process.

Stopping to think breaks the accident chain by activating the M.O.S.T. principles outlined in the chapters you've just read. Just one still moment eliminates distractions, brings you back to awareness of your surroundings, engages your Internal Compass, lets you revisit your past close calls, and most importantly, allows you to make the adjustments and changes in the moment that break the accident chain.

I'll leave you with one last story. My daughter's friend Lucy had recently graduated from nursing school and was running late for her 8:00 a.m. shift one cold, snowy winter morning. With her three kids buckled in and ready to be dropped off at daycare and school, she rushed around her car to scrape the ice off her windshield. She'd only made a few passes across the icy cover when her cheap plastic ice scraper broke into several pieces, littering the driveway. It was freezing, snow was still falling, and the clock was ticking. Shivering outside the vehicle, she could hear her two-year-old screaming in the backseat and her older children bickering over a bottle of orange juice. Even with smooth drop-offs at daycare and school, she'd still be pushing it to get to work on time. Frustrated and stressed, Lucy decided to just turn the defrost on full blast and start driving, peering through a small but slowly growing opening in her windshield, about the size of a basketball.

As she powered through the icy streets of her neighborhood, Lucy was craning her neck forward to see through her tiny window of visibility as the snow kept falling. When she approached the last stop sign before leaving the subdivision, she rolled her windows down just briefly to check for other vehicles and sped off to beat the approaching line of cars. Once on the main road, she soon realized that while she was able to make it through her quiet neighborhood streets well enough with limited visibility, the busy road was another story altogether. She couldn't see other cars around her and could barely see right in front of her through the falling snow. She started to panic.

Lucy paused her racing thoughts and realized how crazy it would be to continue driving like this. In that brief moment, she weighed the consequences of being a few minutes late to work versus the lifelong consequences of an accident that could hurt her children, herself, or someone else. Lucy turned off at the next service station to purchase a two-dollar scraper. After removing the ice completely, she called her supervisor to explain that she would be running a little late. She dropped her kids off safely at daycare and school. She turned on her favorite radio station and took greater care driving down the snowy roads and actually pulled into the parking lot at work at almost the same time she would have on any other day.

That one moment of calm, rational thinking allowed Lucy to check in with her gut and stop stupidity in its tracks. There were links in an accident chain that she couldn't control—like the weather, her children's bickering, and traffic. However, she could control how well she could see through her car's windows. Lucy broke the accident chain by taking a slowdown and scraping the ice off of the car instead of taking the shortcut of driving with impaired visibility; she regained her focus despite the distractions of fighting children and stress over being late. She stopped, thought, and corrected her course. Without that moment of clarity, who knows what could have happened on that icy morning?

Sure, this story might not seem as dramatic as some of the others I've told along the way. In fact, it's pretty boring in comparison, don't you think? Nobody lost a finger or an eye. Nobody died or stuck an antenna up their nose. So why did I include it?

You see, I wish I heard more stories like this. I think it's one of the best ones in the book because Lucy took a slowdown and thus was able to stop, think, and recognize her own accident chain building. Then she took action to break the chain. Lucy is a smart person who was able to stop doing something stupid.

I hope you will be too.

ABOUT THE AUTHOR

Ronald T. Johnston is a respected safety professional, speaker, and author and the founder of Johnston & Associates, Inc., a successful Nashville-based occupational safety and workers' compensation management firm. Having worked with clients from a broad range of industries across the United States, Ron developed the M.O.S.T. system, a behavioral concept that helps employees and supervisors make safety a part of their everyday lives at work and at home.

Ron also created the S.O.S.® system, a defensive driving system used nationally by trucking, manufacturing, distribution, and home healthcare companies to train their employees on the importance of safe driving habits. Ron holds a master's degree from Emory University and has taught business courses at Vanderbilt University's Owen School of Management. He now serves as President of Johnston & Associates, Inc.

An experienced pilot, Ron has accrued more than 1,800 hours of flying over the last twenty years. Aviation is a passion for Ron, offering the perfect mix of sky-high freedom with precision procedures, rules, and regulations. Ron has refined many of the M.O.S.T. principles thanks to lessons he's learned in the cockpit. He currently owns and flies a Bonanza F33A.

Ron and his wife, Carol, live in the Franklin, Tennessee area near their two grown children and their families. They love to travel and spend time with their five grandchildren.

Ron and the Johnston & Associates, Inc. team are available for speaking engagements, safety consulting, and claims management services. Visit JOHNSTONANDASSOC.COM or call 615-373-0500 for more information.